Automating Managers

Automating Managers

The Implications of
Information Technology
for Managers

John Moss-Jones

Pinter Publishers
London and New York
and the
British Institute of Management

© John Moss-Jones 1990

First published in Great Britain in 1990 by
Pinter Publishers Limited
25 Floral Street, London WC2E 9DS

British Library Cataloguing in Publication Data
A CIP catalogue record for this book is available from the
British Library
ISBN 0-86187-837-X

Library of Congress Cataloging in Publication Data
Moss-Jones, John
     Automating managers : the implications of information technology
for managers / John Moss-Jones.
        p.   cm.
     Includes bibliographical references (p.
     ISBN 0–86187–837–X
     1. Business—Data processing—Case studies.   2. Management—Data
processing—Case studies.   3. Information technology—Case studies.
I. Title.
HF5548.2.M6757   1990
658.4′038—dc20   89–25566
                                                                          CIP

Typeset by Acorn Bookwork, Salisbury, Wiltshire
Printed and bound in Great Britain by Biddles Ltd,
Guildford and King's Lynn

Contents

Acknowledgements

My thanks go to the many people who helped me throughout this research: to Roger Evans, Managing Director of Creative Learning Consultants Ltd who started me on the path of the research years ago, and who gave me much wise advice; to Dr David Wield of the Open University who taught and counselled me with such patience and to the members of the OU's Technology Policy Unit for their support and creativity.

The level of cooperation and assistance from the five companies involved was huge—without exception managers unstintingly gave me time from their busy schedules.

And of course I am indebted to Dr Roy Steed, former Director of Luton College of Higher Education, and especially to my colleague-friends in the Centre for Management Studies at Putteridge Bury who constantly helped me maintain momentum in what has been a great learning experience.

1 Introduction

Unfortunately, though practices related to managerial effectiveness are widespread, most are being undertaken without benefit of research-based evidence . . . [Campbell *et al.*, 1970]

Preface

Universally managers are regarded as key to the fortunes of organizations; thus their development is crucial for organizational success, however framed. Effective management development, it is widely argued, hinges on understanding the actual work and contexts of managers, and these are likely to be increasingly affected by information technology (IT).

The principal interest of the author is in the education, training and development of managers. Hence, the motivation for the research described here is to improve understanding of how IT is influencing organizational contexts of managers and, specifically, how the work, roles and behaviour of managers are changing. The research focused on IT effects but, as will be seen, what emerged is a view of the current nature of manager's work as they wrestle with changing cultures. In the concluding chapter brief suggestions are made about improving management competences in this context.

Technology, society and work

Over the years, the nature and place of technology have been researched extensively from two predominant perspectives: the influences of agents such as government, education, workers and management on the diffusion and use of technology; and the influences of technology on these agents. It is important at the outset to emphasize the two-way interaction between technology (and specifically IT) and any other agent: each is continuously changing and producing new influences on the other. There is a dynamic fabric of causes and effects—a situation common to all social research and a fundamental reason for the difficulties of method and of understanding. The research described in this book focuses on a *one-directional* influence: of IT on managers. Nevertheless the complexity and interactivity of the organizational fabric is present always.

All happenings have precursors, and although public awareness of IT had a dramatic upturn in the late 1970s (Jenkins and Sherman, 1979), research interest in computers and their interplay within organizations has been ongoing for decades (Leavitt and Whisler, 1957; Beer, 1959; Whisler, 1966; Stewart, 1971). As in the general case of technology and its interaction with other elements, research into computing (and later into IT) and its reciprocal relationships has concentrated mainly on the influences on the diffusion of the technology and on the effects of the technology on selected actors, mainly shop-floor workers, and on control of their work. For instance, Armstrong (1984) looked at technical change and reduction in life hours of labour at work, and Bell (1983) reported on the behaviour of labour in situations of technical change and on the competitive weakness of British manufacturing. Hartman *et al.* (1983) examined the use of computerized machine tools and their effects on manpower and skills utilization in the differing cultural and structural contexts of British and West German manufacturing firms, a theme further explored by Bessant and Grunt (1985). In fact, the literature on the management of technical change is characterized not by the impact of technical change on managers or management, the subject of this book, but by its prescriptions of how managers should plan, organize and control new technologies for the use of others.

But IT has one characteristic which both separates it quite distinctly from technologies in general and makes it of central importance to managers. It deals with information—the quintessential stuff of organizations and management. Whereas technology until now has mainly been applied to physical processes, thereby mostly affecting shop-floor workers and activities, IT operates on and within the information patterns and processes of organizations and is thus at the heart and brain of management itself.

Managerial work

Although there is a vast management literature, the nature of managerial work is still not well understood. For example Campbell *et al.* (1970) summed up their extensive literature study as follows:

Much of the business and psychological literature on the topic of managerial effectiveness is based on little more than personal experiences or opinions about 'traits' possessed by good managers, what they must do to be effective, or what the products of their effective behaviour may be . . . [p. 15] Unfortunately, though practices related to managerial effectiveness are widespread, most are being undertaken without benefit of research-based evidence defining the nature and effects of determiners of managerial effectiveness. [p. 4]

Though that was written years ago, there is little evidence in the literature that the situation has changed. It is not surprising, therefore, that the management literature is even more sparse on influences of IT on management work.

Here then is a paradox. It is well accepted that organizational well-being, however defined, is predominantly dependent on management, and that IT is likely to be a powerful influence on organizational information and decision processes—both central to management. Yet, to date, the influence of IT on the work, roles and behaviour of managers has received little research attention. Consequently, understanding of this interaction is not well documented as is shown by the wide-ranging survey of research by Friedman (1983) undertaken for the SSRC (now ESRC).

Themes in the literature

Because of inherent qualities, described later, IT has wide applicability and is entering organizations in many forms: for instance on the shop floor through robotics and automation; in offices via computers and between sites in the form of telecommunications. This versatility and ubiquity implies effects both local in space and time and non-direct. The latter are those extending to features distant from the site of the IT application, often having consequences well after the application took place. Wilkinson (1982), for instance, emphasizes the learning which goes on long after a microelectronics system is introduced in manufacturing; Friedman (1985) confirms the same in data-processing installations. Dawson and McLoughlin (1984) point out structural changes hierarchically distant from the applications of computer technology in freight handling.

We are thus dealing with the interactions of two complex fields: information technology, which actually comprises several interwoven technologies, and managerial work. To understand this interaction it is necessary to review, and to draw upon, a wide literature particularly covering:

- The nature, development, application and diffusion of technology generally, and information technology in particular. This tends to divide itself into the *influence* of agents on the technology, and the *implications* of the technology for those agents.

- The nature of work, roles and behaviours of managers. This is set within a voluminous literature on all aspects of management and organizational studies.
- Systems theory and practice. This is itself a large field, and often seems to be separate from, rather than a part of, the management literature.

By and large, these are often treated as separate themes, but they are strongly interactive and must be integrated here in order to make sense of the implications of IT for managers.

Organization of the book

As mentioned earlier, there has not been a strong research emphasis on IT effects on managers. The work described here is undertaken as some contribution to filling this gap. However, the book does not pretend to be comprehensive in its coverage of IT applications and their effects on managerial work. Rather, the research is exploratory and attempts to identify the tendencies for change in managers' work, roles and behaviour as IT increasingly enters their contexts. For reasons set out in chapter three, on method, the five companies studied are all in manufacturing. Nevertheless, the main emphasis is on IT in office settings in a wide range of organizational functions and covering all levels of management.

Chapter two presents an analysis of material relevant to these issues under the following headings:

- The organizational context: the complex cultural, structural and process contexts of organizations that managers deal with and in which IT is being implemented.
- Technology and change—the general case: the nature of the diffusion, usage and consequences of technology in general.
- Information technology: the historical development of IT from its precursors and its generic characteristics.
- Management processes and systems: organizational processes and systems, and specifically those considered to be managerial.
- The implications framework: for use in acquiring data from field work and for its subsequent analysis.

Chapter three describes the thinking leading to the choice of the five manufacturing companies studied, and the interview, questionnaires and other data-collection methods used. Chapter four sets out the findings of the field work in case-study form. Within the thesis resulting from the research, this field-work material is written up in a very detailed way with many quotations from interviewees. These case studies have been much condensed in this book, but it is hoped that the key ideas are preserved. Chapter five examines and integrates thematically the data from the five companies. Chapter six summarizes the conclusions of the research and considers their relevance to management and management development. At the outset the main questions appeared to be:

(1) What is the character of IT diffusion and implementation in the companies?
(2) How is IT changing the general nature of managerial work?
(3) How are specific components of managers' work, namely communication, decision making and interpersonal matters, being affected?
(4) To what extent are the implications of IT on managers dependent on existing management practices and cultures?

These research questions have stimulated and guided, hopefully in a creative way, the literature study, the field work and the subsequent analysis.

Finally, it should be noted that the research focuses on the work and behaviour of *managers* as individual role-holders, although naturally *management*, the composite of these roles as a cultural, structural and process entity within the organizations, is referred to where relevant. Also, the term 'administration' is generally avoided since in British industry and commerce it has connotations of lower-order clerical work. 'Management' here is taken to mean the organizational executive hierarchy inclusive of supervisors.

2 Information technology and managers

The impact of new technology depends on where and how it is used. The wide range of application leads to a similarly wide range of effects, many of which may be in different directions . . . [Sorge *et al.*, 1982]

Organizational contexts are highly complicated, and as the literature consistently illustrates, the diffusion, usage and implications of technology are equally so. IT is entering virtually all aspects of companies and is thus impinging upon key organizational processes—the work, roles and behaviour of managers.

The organizational context

Information technology is impacting upon managers within the immensely complex contexts of organizations. Groups of people transacting among themselves, and with other individuals and groups beyond their own boundaries, involve many forces—social, psychological, political, economic, technological—each continuously modifying and changing its influence on the others and on the whole organization. These aspects of organizations have been extensively researched for decades; the literature is huge and rich, but confusing. 'The domain of organization theory is coming to resemble a weed-patch—researchers confront an almost bewildering array of variables, perspectives, and inferred prescriptions' (Pfeffer, 1982). Similarly Engwall (1982) wrote: 'The goal of a unified organization theory has not been achieved and it seems less likely today than 70 years ago.'

This section presents an analysis of the organizational context in which managers work and within which IT is impacting. Since IT comprises several technologies and applications, it is important to understand that there are a multitude of IT effects interacting with many, and various, organizational features.

Classification of the literature can only be arbitrary for, while there are 'schools', their definitions and boundaries, within organizational theory alone are (as Pfeffer wrote) bewildering. But the situation is even more complicated. For in order to understand the implications of IT for the work of managers, it is necessary to look at three terrains, which have often been treated as separate: technology, the work of managers and systems. As already stated, these themes are contiguous and interactive.

Organizations will be treated here as having three predominant features: culture, structure and processes.

Organizational culture

Culture is the unwritten sets of assumptions and expectations which organizational members hold, and which give meaning to their own and others' actions (Handy, 1976). Recently, greater emphasis has been placed on the ways in which organizational cultures maintain themselves over time (Deal and Kennedy, 1982) and in relation to change (Pettigrew *et al.*, 1982; Mintzberg, 1984). Naturally, there are many sub-cultures within an organization (for instance, of manual workers, research and development or marketing), but in this book the focus is on management sub-culture.

Organizational structure

Structure, according to Child (1977) allocates people and resources to tasks, and provides mechanisms for their coordination, for indicating expectations to staff and for decision-taking. This description incurs difficulties, for like some other authors, Child includes in structure specifications of *processes*. Nevertheless, structure is the relatively visible descriptions and prescriptions of the patterns of tasks, responsibilities, authority and roles (Dalton *et al.*, 1970).

Structure is *form* and defines:

1. The number of roles and their titles (for instance, one sales director, five regional sales managers, 26 salespersons).
2. The functional groupings of staff and responsibilities—the generic 'horizontal' divisions of a company: for instance marketing, finance, production, personnel and their subdivisions. Marketing might be subdivided into advertising, direct sales, technical support, though, as we shall see, each company is unique in structuring and naming functions.

3. The hierarchical 'vertical' responsibility patterns—the number of 'tiers' and the 'spans of command'.
4. The tasks, responsibilities, authority and status of individual roles. The degree to which these definitions exist in any organization varies enormously and is itself part of that specific culture.
5. Various committees, communication and decision patterns—again specific to each particular organization (Litterer, 1965; Miller and Rice, 1967).

In this book the term 'designatory' structure is used to encompass 1–5 above.

Structural-contingency theory has probably been the dominant approach in the sociological and business school literatures, with the assumption that an element of the organization's context, for instance technology, produces certain structural consequences (Woodward, 1965; Pugh *et al.*, 1968). As will be shown later, this idea is confirmed: IT is changing organizational structures.

According to Cowling and Evans (1985), in the United Kingdom there is little formal organizational design in companies: structures are based on the experience of senior managers and on issues of head-count pressure. The relationship of structure to culture, and to processes is generally not widely considered, at least in British organizations. It seems that structure is decided by individuals, or groups, and is characterized by 'state' discretion, ie most of the features of structure are in state A until at a particular moment they change to state B. Exceptions to this would be the degree of definition of managers' roles and responsibilities, which might alter gradually. Managers patently vary in the extent to which they will conform to any formal, or even implied, definition of their roles or allow variation from role definition in their subordinates.

Organizational processes

Processes are *ongoing* within the organization, and across its external boundaries, and are thus characterized by activity. They vary widely from shop-floor production, for instance manual handling of products or equipment, to intellectual processes such as decision making, or interpersonal ones as in interviewing. Processes may be 'management' processes or 'non-management' processes dependent on levels of discretion and responsibility. The literature on all processes is abundant and often presents them as *systems*, or sub-systems (for instance Beer, 1959, 1972; Thompson, 1967; Kast and Rosenzweig, 1979).

It is quite common to describe the cluster of linked operations of a manufacturing company (such as machining, assembly, inventory, quality and associated planning and control mechanisms) as the production system. Likewise 'information system' or 'communication system' is usually used to mean the flow of information throughout the organization and beyond its boundaries.

While systems are usually associated with processes, which imply flows of, for instance artefacts (the production system), money (the banking system), people (a transportation system), the same characterization is used for data (management information system), or a complete organization or society. In these latter more global situations, 'system' may be used to include structure or culture as well as processes.

The primacy of management processes

Twentieth-century civilization is a society of organizations, and the leadership groups of old, often based on aristocracy or religion, have been replaced by managers according to Drucker (1982). Within all organizations there are certain prime processes which are specifically managerial in nature—setting goals, establishing, assigning and coordinating resources, monitoring achievement (and others). Organizational politics are not part of this book, but it is noteworthy that there is always an ongoing struggle for power between various actors in organizations, about control of key processes, and this is always an element in the culture specific to each organization, not least in the arena of technology (Wilkinson, 1983). It is important to note that this struggle is not unitary opposition of management and non-management, but rather an often paradoxical amalgam of conflict and cooperation amongst a 'web of interests' (Cressey and McInnes, 1980).

'Management' then is, by general agreement, the primary subset in the organization viewed as a system. Beer sees it as 'the brain of the firm'; Kast and Rosenzweig (1979) as one of five subsystems; the others being goals and values, structural, psychosocial and technological, all interconnected by the managerial subsystem. There is also wide consensus among both researchers and practitioners that information transactions are fundamental to all processes in organizations (Galbraith, 1977; Hay and Majluf, 1981). Inter-relatedness, the coupling between relevant organizational activities, is a prime function of management and is also dependent upon the quality and quantity of information transactions. Both management processes and information transactions (the arena of IT) are then intimately associated with organizational competence and relative success. (It is interesting that *inter-relatedness* within nature (Capra, 1975; Russell, 1982) and within societies (Williams, 1981 and 1983), as well as within organizations, is simultaneously emerging as an important issue.)

Classically, the early literature presented some sort of management principles which were thought to be universally or at least widely applicable. Fayol (1916) divided management into planning, organizing, motivating, coordinating and controlling, and he was followed along similar lines by Barnard (1938) and Brech (1953). Until very recently, authors seemed compelled to classify all aspects of organizations and management into highly defined and tightly boundaried compartments. The more systems-oriented approach of Beer (1959) and Miller and Rice (1967) softened the functional boundaries and the divisions and began to suggest management was an integrating function.

But there is another element weakening the concreteness and compartmentalized approach of management writing. While the flows of artefacts, and money in organizations, and the visible manifestations of structure, were amenable to study, the work, roles and behaviours of managers have proved almost impossible to observe and analyse unequivocally. In practice the theoretical Fayolian processes merge one with another, and often go on simultaneously. Planning for instance can be at the same time coordination or motivation. The more empirically based authors, for instance Lorsch and Allen (1973), emphasize appropriateness rather than adherence to formula. Particular management approaches derive from, or are relevant to, specific organizational contexts. Burns and Stalker (1961), for example held that fast change led to 'organic', while slower change had 'mechanistic' management styles, a conclusion especially pertinent to the research here described.

Technology in organizations

The effects of technology in organizations has been studied by the early management observers (Taylor, 1911; Gantt, 1919; Gilbreth, 1920). Originally, all work had been carried out virtually exclusively by people, using tools as appropriate, but machines have been taking over this work in an uneven manner, temporally and spatially, depending on technological invention, development, diffusion and usage. The early writers mentioned above, and others, saw machines primarily as entering the production (and transport) functions; machine power and manipulative efficacy substituting for human muscle and skill. The effects therefore were principally upon manual shop-floor workers. Although there were obvious concomitant changes in labour processes, floor layouts and emphasis, the impingement on managers was peripheral. The fundamental processes in which managers took major roles remained essentially the same.

Although Woodward (1958 and 1965), Khandwala (1974) and others found type and degree of technology to be contingent for management features, principally structure, the research was almost exclusively looking at technology on the shop floor. Technology was being used within data-handling functions in telephonic and telex communications and in punched card systems before 1950, and there were many studies of these (Shannon and Weaver, 1949; Cherry, 1957). But it is only since 1959 that computers have been used in business and then to begin with, only in a discrete, isolated 'main-frame' mode, generally dealing with high-volume, low-'intelligence' processing. In contrast IT since the late 1970s has been entering the central realm of managers: information and communication systems and decision making. Further, this later phase of IT is leading to a distributed network mode and is able to deal with higher levels of complexity.

To summarize, a number of themes have been described in this section:

• Organizations can be seen as culture, structure and processes and their interaction.
• Processes, and to an extent, everything in organizations can be described in system terms.
• Management is a primary sub-system.
• Information transactions are fundamental in organizational processes and to management.
• Management is holistic and integrating and uses information in this key role.
• Until the late 1970s, although technology was important within organizations, it had only tangential effects on managers.
• Information technology is now entering the central realm of managers: information and communication systems and decision making.

The relationships between culture, structure, processes and IT are depicted in Figure 2.1, below. Note that processes can be 'management' or 'non-management' and both are influenced by IT.

Technology and change: the general case

Before looking at IT, it is useful to consider the general case of technology and change in organizations. As Schumpeter (1954) pointed out:

Long before the industrial revolution, people realized the obvious fact that machinery often displaces labor . . . Governments and writers worried about this and labor groups and citizens' guilds fought against machinery, the more so because immediate effects of this kind are concentrated in time and place, whereas the long run effects on general wealth are much less visible in the short run and much less easy to trace to the machine.

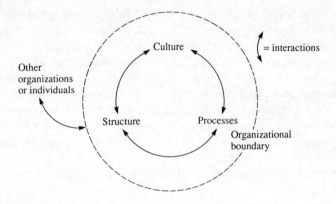

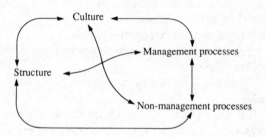

Processes can be seen as either management or non-management:

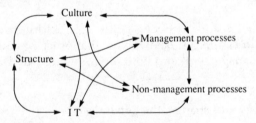

IT is entering both non-management, and management processes:

Figure 2.1   Relationship between culture, structure and processes

Technological influences

The long history of technological applications has brought change to organizations, workers, management and society, and has been the focus of attention of economic historians such as Toynbee (1908), Cunningham (1903) and the Webbs (1932). Nevertheless, according to Mathias (1983) most attention was given to the consequences—and usually adverse consequences—on society generally, rather than on the specific implications in organizations. Within the literature there has tended to be an heroic tradition of ascribing great and specific import-ance to particular inventors and to their inventions (the Watt engine, Hargreaves' spinning jenny are examples), whereas recent studies (Schmookler, 1966; Parker, 1972; Rosenberg, 1976; Williams, 1983 and Ray, 1983) have revealed processes of innovation and diffusion to be much more gradual, evolutionary and anonymous. This is an important conclusion to bear in mind in consideration of IT and its implications within organizations.

Britain's relative industrial decline has been a cause of concern for a century or more, and many explanations have been forthcoming, most of which have included the lacklustre British performance in *developing* and *using* technologies (Hobsbawn, 1968; Lewis, 1978; Pavitt, 1980 and Wiener, 1981). In contrast it has been widely accepted that in scientific research Britain has been pre-eminent (though Irvine and Martin (1984) have recently suggested that British research has been less efficacious for the national economy than was commonly believed). The vast literature on this issue establishes the complexity, and the interdepend-ence, of the many variables associated with technology and Britain's economic development. It is clear that the problems are not so much specifically scientific, or even technological, but multi-factored and human (Swann, 1983). Much of this literature deals with technical, economic, government policy, labour market and societal issues (Bessant *et al.*, 1981; Bell, R. M., 1983; Williams, 1983; Liff, 1983).

Typically the research considers how the diffusion of innovations is influenced by various social, economic or policy components, or how technology affects such elements as productivity, wage differentials and employment in various market sectors or industries. It is worth repeat-ing that in this research tradition there is relatively little looking at the effects of technology on managers, or on managements. Further, although management is patently the vital agency in organizations, the influence of management on technology diffusion and usage has also received scant treatment.

Science has always been allowed to be conceptual, even though much practice is clearly involved, but technology has a stronger connotation of doing, and is often a synonym for machinery. Yet it is quite possible for technology to involve no machines at all. Schumpeter (1939) described technological change as 'any "doing things differently" in the realm of economic life', and certainly in every technological change there is much that is conceptual, organizational, economic and managerial.

It is plain then that changes in technology, broadly defined, have had profound effects on societies at several levels, both in its immediate impact, and in its gradual consequences (Macdonald, 1983). Although, taking a historical perspective, it is now easy to see, for instance, the effects on transport of the steamship and of the airplane, *at the time* it seems to be extremely difficult to understand what is actually happening.

Technology and work

Within organizations from Taylor (1911) on, changes in the formaliza-tion of labour work, and later 'mechanization' (Bright, 1958) altered physical layouts, labour groupings and certain control functions of management. Technology was being applied almost exclusively in pro-duction functions, and most directly affected factors related to that function (Child and Mansfield, 1972). Woodward (1965) conceptualized technology in production into three types: small batch, large batch, and continuous process, and based her analysis therefore on periodicity of the production process. She found that several organizational character-istics were related to these types such as the ratios of managers to total personnel, of clerical and administrative staff to manual workers, the labour cost as a proportion of turnover and the span of control of the chief executives.

The Aston Studies (Hickson *et al.*, 1969; Pugh *et al.*, 1976) however, failed to replicate Woodward's results on the importance of technology. Indeed, in spite of the volume of work in this field, there are few clear conclusions: '. . . the discrepancies . . . seem to be at least as great as the commonalities' (Child and Mansfield, 1972). Inconsistency within the literature may be caused by the lack of common conceptual defini-tion and different levels of analysis (Gerwin, 1979). Various authors adopt different conceptualizations of technology—for instance Perrow (1967) sees technology as work done on raw materials, a characterization linking technology essentially with the production function common to many writers before about 1970 (see also Woodward, 1958).

Indeed the greater part of research and writing about organizations, specifically in relation to the implications of technology, took place with this kind of characterization, certainly before what is now termed information technology was introduced on a significant scale.

Also, predominantly, researchers focused on organizational (and usually structural) and labour process implications, and relatively little attention was given to effects on managers. Following the work of Sorge *et al.* (1983), Mansfield (1984) suggests a number of trends widely observed in work organizations, and typical of the writings in this arena including increases in:

(1) Mechanization of work leading to replacement of human effort by machines and technical systems.
(2) Automation of work leading to the replacement of human thinking and control by machines and technical systems.

(3) Capital intensity leading to a partial replacement of labour costs by investment in machines and technical systems, and more obviously by a shift in the balance of expenditure, thus decreasing the percentage spent on wages and salaries.

(4) Division of labour between different functional activities. This is seen both between different personnel involved directly in the production process, and between production activities and control, support and other staff activities.

(5) Polarization of skills leading to a very sharp and significant gap in the skills, experience and qualifications between largely semi-skilled operatives and the frequently highly technically skilled design, control and maintenance personnel.

(6) Centralization of decision making relating to operating decisions.

(7) Bureaucratization of production with increasing use of plans and schedules.

Mansfield suggests that these trends can be explained in terms of dealing with task accomplishment and cost control or reduction, and that maintaining managerial control is largely a secondary problem the solution to which is instrumental in finding solutions to the other two issues.

In the general case then, technology, a broad mix of machines, concepts and techniques, has diffused in a largely gradual, evolutionary, anonymous and patchy fashion. And as we shall see later, the same is true for IT. Although in retrospect the implications of technological change seem obvious to authors, they are complex, often contradictory and almost incomprehensible at the time the technological change is occurring. That technology is an important sub-system of organizations is well understood (Kast and Rosenzweig, 1979), but agreement within the literature about its implications for organizations only holds at general levels and has mostly not focused on implications for managers.

Information technology

Information technology follows the general trends of technology but is postulated here to be a special case because it is dealing with information and because it is directly entering the managerial realm. In many ways information technology is only a sub-set of the general case of technology, though because it is related to the quintessential stuff of society, information, it is argued widely that it has a special nature and importance.

A long evolution of artefacts, processes and ideas characterize the development of IT: signal fires, flags, the abacus, stagecoach mail, maps, codes, mathematics—all significant in human history (Singer *et al.*, 1954; Dummer, 1977; Strandh, 1979; Maddison, 1983). And since the nineteenth century there has been an acceleration in electrical and electronic developments, which led to a burgeoning after, say, 1930, of a matrix of data-processing concepts and hardware: the telephone, radio, radar, sonar, machine coding, punched card machines and computers (Toothill, 1965).

Early days in computing

The first computers operated as discrete, central, rather isolated machines, and although able to manipulate large amounts of relatively simple data quickly, were not integrated into the organization as a whole. As these 'mainframe' computers came into common use in the 1950s and 1960s, predictions were widespread that the effects would be 'revolutionary' for organizational structures and processes. Leavitt and Whisler (1957) predicted a return to centralized decision making and a considerable reduction in middle-management staff, as decision making moved upward and computers took over the information processing roles of such staff. Whisler (1966) found five major effects:

- Decision making can be rationalized, with a greater access to quantified information;
- Enlarged scope of decisions since more information is available;
- Level at which decisions are made may change;
- Rhythm of planning decisions may change;
- Decisions made by man–machine, and not just man–man systems.

Rosemary Stewart (1971), in her well-known studies of computers in several companies (four of which were in manufacturing) concluded:

- Effects on management varied from one case to another;
- The type of computer application influenced the nature of the effects on management;
- The effects on management varied within the same type of application;
- The effects of computer applications on management were not inevitable;
- During the computerization process the most common effect is an increased workload for managers;
- Managers (in one case) appeared to make more use of the system with time;
- The most striking effect was the way managers were stimulated by the use of computers to think about their policies and activities;
- Organizationally the main effect was the creation of a computer department;
- There was a marked decrease in clerical staff, and sometimes an elimination of one tier;

- An increase in formalization of procedures took place;
- There was no evidence of increased centralization;
- Levels at which decisions were taken may be changed;
- Time horizons may change;
- Power balance between departments may change;
- Department boundaries may be weakened.

An American study at about the same time (Churchill *et al.*, 1969), based on interviews with users, managers and computer department management in several companies, concluded that the information systems literature presented a far more advanced picture than that which actually existed (a point worth keeping in mind in a field well noted for hyperbole). The researchers found there was little or no impact on higher levels of management.

These pieces of research are illustrative of much of the literature before the late 1970s. They describe centralized, isolated, 'undistributed' computing, usually with a single computer under the control of an 'electronic data processing' department. The researchers varied widely in their analyses, and their predictions, from the Whisler model of revolutionary change, to the Stewart and Churchill conclusions which were more grounded and tentative. Significantly it is difficult to find any anticipation in the management literature before 1978 of the dramatic developments in microelectronics which were about to become public. For instance, it is given but a few lines in the report of a major colloquium on 'the changing expectations of society in the next thirty years' held at Windsor Castle in 1979 by the American Assembly of Collegiate Foundation for Management Development. In the report of an international seminar in La Hulpe, Belgium, February 1978, 'Management Education in the 1980's' there is no mention of information technology—in fact the word 'computer' occurs only once!

The arrival of IT

Almost certainly in the United Kingdom the public awakening—and government reaction to it—sprang from the BBC TV 'Horizon' programme 'Now The Chips Are Down' in the Spring of 1979, and its text which appeared in the *Listener* on 6 April that year. Notwithstanding its long evolution, suddenly IT became recognized by the major nations as a considerable factor in contemporary economic and social dynamics. In fact, throughout the Western world there began a period of intense interest in IT with an outpouring of literature and media comment, much of it predicting substantial changes in society, in organizations and in work (Nora and Minc, 1978; Jenkins and Sherman, 1979; Barron and Curnow, 1979; Bessant, 1981; Friedrichs and Schaff, 1982; Gershuny and Miles, 1983). Japan, the United States, Europe and the United

Kingdom quickly set up large-scale research projects into the technology and its applications.

In spite of the predictions, since the late 1970s, 'It is apparent that the available evidence is too scant for commentators to find common ground' (Land in Piercy (ed.), 1984). Sorge *et al.* (1982): 'A great number of studies have been carried out, which deal with microelectronics as a general phenomenon and try to determine economic and social consequences. However, no reliable assessment of the impact has been possible.'

Two schools of thought about IT are articulated within the literature. The first might be termed the 'rationalists', for they see IT as part of the continuing and inevitable substitution of machines, albeit electronic now, rather than mechanical as in the past, for people, and so derive directly from the Taylor tradition. This viewpoint is often termed 'deterministic' in the literature. The school might be divided into optimists and pessimists. The optimists believe that the technology is neutral or favourable (Baker, 1980; Evans, 1979) and will result in improved social, and economic consequences and especially more effective management (Kearney, 1984). The pessimists believe the process will inevitably result in an increase in social controls, degradation of work and reduction in jobs (Braverman, 1974; Barron and Curnow, 1979; Jenkins and Sherman, 1979).

The second school takes a contingency approach (Bessant and Grunt, 1985; Land in Piercy (ed.), 1984) and is probably well summed up by Sorge *et al.* (1982):

The impact of new information technology depends on where and how it is used. The wide range of application leads to a similarly wide range of effects, many of which may be in different directions. We would argue . . . that the consistent references to microelectronics having 'effects' is not helpful.

One question then for the field work was to what extent were the implications of IT for managers contingent on the character of their situations and their organizational context.

The character of IT

The definition of IT adopted by Unesco, is 'the scientific, technological and engineering disciplines and the management techniques used in information handling and processing; their applications; computers and their interaction with men and machines; and associated social, economic and cultural matters' (Raitt, 1982). A more practical description was given by Kenneth Baker, the first British Minister of State for Industry and Information Technology in 1982: 'The use of computers, microelectronics and telecommunications to help us produce, obtain and send information in the form of pictures, words or numbers, more reliably, quickly and economically'.

COMPUTER GENERATIONS

Computer technology has moved through a number of 'generations' categorized by hardware characteristics as follows:

1st generation (1940s and 1950s)
Thermionic valve-based central processing unit (CPU), rotating memory, un-developed software; used mainly in scientific work, and later in accounting, invoicing and payroll applications at the same time as Hollerith punched-card machines.

2nd generation (late 1950s to mid-1960s)
Transistors in CPU, magnetic core memory; software compilers and languages introduced; basically batch processors, computers become common in large organizations.

3rd generation (mid-1960s to mid-1970s)
Large-scale integrated circuits (LSI) for CPUs; developing real-time processing, and on-line applications by remote terminals; programming routine and skilled; later, semi-conductor technology for main memory, and time sharing using 'virtual memory'.

4th generation (mid-1970s to date)
Very large-scale integrated circuits (VLSI); increased power for size; very large fast semi-conductor memories; on-line applications for large data bases. IT emerges: convergence with telecommunications; microcomputers; very fast hardware cost reduction; new programming languages; user-friendliness.

5th generation (1990? to ?)
Higher-scale component integration: one micron, and later sub-micron geo-metrics (10,000 gates/mm^2, or 500,000 gates per chip); parallel computer archi-tectures; improved languages; improved man–machine interfaces, including early speech recognition; intelligent knowledge-based systems increasingly used (Lucas, 1982; Moto-Oka, 1982; Danzin, 1983; Alvey, 1985; Potterdam Conference Papers, 1984; Ennals and Cotterell, 1985).

ELECTRONIC DATA PROCESSING

While it would not be appropriate in this work to include detailed descriptions of office or shop-floor technologies, understanding of the basic IT equipment and applications is essential to the subsequent discussion. Definitions of both 'data', and 'information' abound, but there is a consensus that data are 'raw', while information is derived from it, has meaning to the recipient and is of value, or perceived value, in decision making. However, in reality the difference between data and information is not always clear, and the words are used almost interchangeably. Note also that the value of information is dependent upon a range of factors. Again, the elements within 'intelligence' (used in the military sense) processes vary according to author, but here will be classified as:

- Data capture
- Data storage
- Data transmission
- Data analysis
- Data reformatting
- Data display (on paper, visual or audio)
- Decision making (machine, or machine/human or human).

These elements may be combined in many ways, but commonly are as shown in Figure 2.2.

IT then is usually some combination of telecommunications and computing, and may also include 'application equipment' such as robotics. *Telecommunications* facilities generally do not change the information content between input and output, and include telephone, radio, telex, electronic mail (e-mail), electronic message handling, facsimile (fax), teleconferencing, audio or audiographic conferencing and data networking (for digital transmission of computer data and images) (Baker, 1980; Doswell, 1983). Telecommunications are now essentially computer based for the timing, routing and formatting of messages and data. In most *computing* facilities, changes in information content may be inherent in the process, though this returns to the meanings of information and data. Computers will here be treated as 'black boxes', but the classification in Figure 2.3 is a guide.

Where IT is used in control engineering, in automation and in robotics, there is always a point at which the 'data management' is translated into physical activity through equipment. Opinions vary as to whether this physical equipment should be regarded as part of IT. This is not an important issue in this book.

There is a general consensus in the literature that IT has generic characteristics which make it different, not only from 'computing' but also from all previous technologies. It is postulated throughout this work that the character of IT influences many aspects of the organization and these are changing managerial work and roles. These *generic characteristics* are now to be analysed and presented here. In essence IT consists of combinations of several technologies all based on electronics, or opto-electronic hardware, incorporating systems principles, being used in many varied applications. The effects of IT in organizations derive from an amalgam of some or all of its characteristics dependent

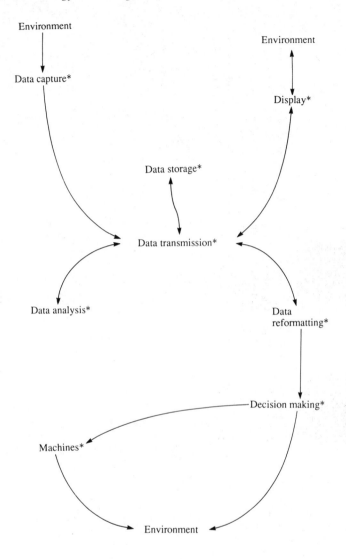

Environment

Data capture*

Environment

Display*

Data storage*

Data transmission*

Data analysis*

Data
reformatting*

Decision making*

Machines*

Environment

*All these could be paper-manual (PM) or could be I T – driven.

Figure 2.2   Data flow

upon applications. This is important; the implications of IT are not due to a single characteristic such as processing speed, though in certain applications this is a prime factor, but to an array of characteristics. As will be shown later, IT has a *field-effect*—interacting with the total system that is the organization, and creating change in culture, structure and processes, but in ways which are contingent upon these three components of the system.

Category	Cost*	Word size (bits)	Main memory	Secondary memory	Floating-point operations per second	Simult. users	Space req'd	Total support staff	Some manufacturers
Supercomputer	$£10^6$	128			10^8	1 or a few		Dozens	Cray, Cyber
Mainframe Very heavy scientific or engineering work, large-scale commercial DP, flight-traffic control, component of continental defence system, dominant node of major network	$£10^5$	64	10+ Mbytes	1 Gbyte	10^6	Many	Suite	Dozens	IBM, Honeywell, NCR, ICL
Mini Scientific or engineering, plant control, CAD, educational multi-user system, large office system, node of wide area network (WAN)	$£10^4$	32	A few Mbytes	100 Mbytes	Many 10^3	20–250 8	Small room	10 2	DEC, HP, GEC, Data General, Harris, Prime, Norsk Data

Micro Personal (professional or home) computer, small office systems, mode of local area network (LAN), laboratory monitoring and control	£10^3	32 16	0.5 Mbytes 100+ Kbytes	10 Mbytes	Some 10^3	4	On or under desk	1 or 2	IBM, DEC, HP, Olivetti, NCR, Apple, ICL, ACT, Amstrad, Atari, Commodore
Programmable calculator	£10^2	8	30 Kbytes	100 Kbytes	10^2	1	Desk	0	Sinclair
Pocket calculator	£20 £5		1 Kbytes 4 bytes	0	1	1 1	Hand Hand	0 0	Tandy, Cassio

Kbyte 1,000 bytes
Mbyte 1,000,000 bytes
Gbyte 1,000,000,000 bytes
*Prices are changing quickly; prices also depend on specification, and what peripheral equipment is included. Note also that all operating characteristics are improving, word bit size, main memory; thus any classification is out of date within three years.

Figure 2.3 Mainframes, minis and micros—a perspective (Walker, 1986)

GENERIC CHARACTERISTICS

Combination—IT is a phrase which has been given to combinations of several technologies, the principal ones being computing, telecommunications, microelectronic and software engineering. In addition there are other technologies—automation, robotics, opto-electronics, lasers and satellites—which are also dependent upon, or associated with IT (see Figure 2.4). Underlying these combinations are the practices of information handling, and the facilitating concept that all data can be converted to a two-stage (binary) form especially suited to electronics, or opto-electronics. This applies to all data sensed directly from the 'physical' world, for instance chemical or biological measurements, and all data from the 'social' world such as numbers of people, hours worked, money spent, costs, items scrapped. These latter may be directly sensed, or may be inputted from people via terminals or paper. (Naturally the physical and social environments are contiguous.)

Once data are in binary form reformatting is intrinsically easy, as is transmission—both at very high speeds. The combinations of technologies are thus possible because of the underlying common information concepts. Whereas previous technologies applied to specific and limited areas—for instance to weaving, coal mining, metal machining or transport, IT is a broad, facilitating technology, likely to be rooted in all future technological developments (Large, 1980 and 1984; Laurie, 1983). Figure

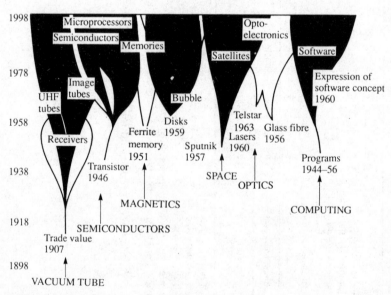

Figure 2.4 Basic elements of IT
Source: Danzin, 1983

2.4 illustrates the basic elements of IT (from Danzin in Otway and Peltu, 1983, p. 22).

Development rapidity—IT has been characterized by a rapidity of development far in excess of any previous technology. Figure 2.5 gives an array of data comparing computers from 1959 and 1984. Figure 2.6 shows speed and cost comparisons for hardware for first through fourth generations.

Danzin (1983) suggests that between 1960 and 1980 there has been a ten-thousandfold improvement in key aspects of IT such as volume and weight per performance, operating speed, price reduction and energy consumption.

Military applications are continuing to be important for IT. This stimulates huge government expenditure in the field. In addition the

	1959	1984
Machine	Pegasus	ICL
Status	Medium performance per cost	Personal computer low performance
Price (1984 equivalent)	£750,000	£2,000
Processor working store	375 packages 1 Kbytes	1 card 250 Kbytes
Permanent store	Magnetic drums 42K + Magnetic tape 100K	5¼-inch disc = 500K
Typical environment	Air-conditioned computer room	Desk top anywhere
Performance	3K instructions per second	1,000K instructions per second
Power consumption	13.5 kW	.280 kW
Weight	900 kg	16 kg
Price/byte of working store	£750,000	£8
Price/K instructions per second	£250,000	£2
Price/K immediate permanent store	£17,825	£4

Figure 2.5 Comparison of computers: 1959 and 1984
Source: Watson, 1985

Generation	Access time per digit (microsecs)	Binary add time (microsecs)	Two-digit add per hour (millions)	Cost per million two-digit adds (US cents)
1st (1950s)	10	700	51.4	35
2nd (1961)	4.5	88	409	5.56
3rd (1965)	.63	12	2,400	1.25
3.5 (1971)	.19	4.2	6,792	.54
4th (1979)	.11	3.4	8,372	.13

Figure 2.6   Hardware generations: speed and cost comparisons
Source: Lucas, 1982, p. 243.

commercial market for IT is vast, continuing to grow quickly and motivating research and development funding. The Japanese 'Fifth Generation' (Moto-Oka, 1982), the British 'Alvey' (Alvey, 1985), the European ESPRIT, FAST (FAST, 1984) and several American research and development programmes are consequences of the competitive IT scene. The literature of the history of technology shows that contemporary views of particular inventions or developments are varied and often wrong. Whether the present extremely fast pace of IT development will be seen historically as a special phenomenon of these technologies remains to be seen. However, as will be discussed later, IT has certainly developed and diffused rapidly, and technical development seems certain to continue at a fast pace.

Universality—deriving from common underlying information concepts and practices, IT appears to have extremely wide applications and is currently being used in organizations in the following forms (though applications are not discrete—a particular application may include elements from more than one form):

1. On the 'shop floor' in manufacturing associated with and usually inherent in automation, robots, 'flexible-manufacturing systems', and 'computer-integrated manufacturing'. Applications may include combinations of automatic tool selection, component and sub-assembly movement and machining (March, 1984), and/or robotics (Towill, 1984), all with many management implications (Voss, 1986).
2. In continuous production processes. Starting in 1957, most early computer control systems were in the petrochemical, the steel, and power generation industries because of their common character of high level of fixed assets and twenty-four-hour operation and subsequently spread to paper, cement and glassmaking. Computers are

used to monitor product and equipment status, to provide information for decision making, either by the equipment (for altering equipment states) or by management (Constable, 1971).

3. In a wide variety of 'administrative' functions, usually office based such as inventory control, purchasing, finance and marketing which, until perhaps twenty years ago, were virtually all *paper–manual* (PM) processes (Barras and Swann, 1983; Long, 1984).

4. In various forms of telecommunication between people, offices, and sites, including internationally, allowing data to be transmitted rapidly, often in seconds, with optical fibres, for instance, capable of carrying over 1,000 million bits per second. The literature emphasizes the convergence of telecommunications and computing technologies (Danzin, 1983; Baker, 1980).

5. In systems which aid, or substitute for, management decision making, varying from 'decision support systems' (offering a range of data-base interrogation, and/or modelling) (Lucas, 1982) up to 'intelligent knowledge-based systems (IKBS or 'expert systems') which potentially offer powerful decision aid, for instance in diagnostic situations (Feigenbaum, 1980).

This universality of IT is likely to influence all organizations, and all elements in organizations (Bell, 1973; Porat, 1976; Bannon *et al.*, 1982; Senker, 1984).

Economic advantage—the prices of IT products have been falling rapidly. According to Watson (1985) the cost/performance ratio has improved 100,000,000 times in the twenty-five years from 1959 to 1984. The reduction in hardware costs has been 40 per cent per year during the 1970s (Large, 1984). Software is not considered to be falling in price, indeed according to some authors (for instance Danzin, 1983) is growing in cost. However, consideration of software costs must take into account the increasing complexity of IT applications, and the increasing 'user-friendliness' of software, both of which increase cost of software, but may still produce overall economic advantages within the application. Also, much research into 'fully automated' programming is underway, which will almost certainly begin to reduce software costs (ALVEY, 1986). Certainly, the proportion of costs absorbed by software has been rising: in 1955 software represented less than 20 per cent of total system costs, by 1970 the split was 50–50, and by 1980 software represented 80 per cent of all costs (Tricker, 1982). Nevertheless, there is wide consensus that overall economics are assisting the IT diffusion.

Size of equipment—early computers consisted of racks of thermionic valves (a lamplike device of forty to sixty cm^3 in volume), perhaps 4,000 of them, housed in air-conditioned cabinets filling a large room (Maddison,

1983). There has been a steady size reduction of components using large-scale integration (LSI) and very large-scale integration (VLSI) and 100,000 gates per chip are now common. Research towards 500,000 gates/chip is well advanced (ALVEY, 1985). Computer overall sizes have reduced proportionately and as Watson shows a 16 kg machine in 1984 was much more powerful and faster than the 900 kg 'computer room' machine of 1959. The personal, desk-top, carryable micro-computer is the direct consequence of size reduction, but size advantages also accrue in many 'shop-floor' applications.

Speed of operation—fundamental to micro-electronics is speed of operation, which is measured in thousand-millionths of a second, nanoseconds or million-millionths of a second, picaseconds. (At these speeds the contents of the Bible could be scanned in 1.5 seconds (Large, 1984).) The increase in processing speed is shown in Figure 2.6. Processing speeds are expected to continue to increase using higher component densities, architectural parallelism and higher efficiency software (Simons, 1983), particularly because of the competitive commercial and military pressures like those of the Strategic Defence Initiative.

Speed is important in organizational settings in two ways: first, in *manipulating* and *reformatting* data—millions of times faster than paper–manual arrangements and second, in data *transmissions* throughout the organization and beyond.

Data accessibility—because of data transmission speeds, the relative cheapness of terminals and the decreasing cost of connectibility, the number of access points to data networks is increasing in organizations. In early computer applications the processing machine was 'isolated' from the organization, and transacted via intermediate input and output arrangements, for instance by punched card. The few terminals were located adjacent to the machine and used solely by data processing operators, a cadre special to that function. Batch entry was predominant, that is data was converted from paper into an input medium for the computer and subsequently entered into the machine. Batch entry together with the scarcity of terminals outside the province of the management information systems (MIS) function implied difficulty of access for most staff or managers, with control of MIS in the hands of a special group of managers and operators. As terminals became more widely distributed in the organization a much greater population is able to transact with data networks. Data accessibility is increasing as will be discussed in the fieldwork chapter (chapter four).

System specificity—a computer system is specifically programmed, and will repeatedly and faithfully follow the required procedures on cue. At lower levels of complexity, as with wages calculation procedures, or robot guidance, there is high system specificity.

Many processes in organizations (for instance inventory control) have previously either been entirely paper–manual (PM), or partly PM and partly machine systematic. As these 'intermediate complexity' processes are increasingly computerized, all inputs and relationships have to be reduced to numerical values. The processes themselves have to be analysed, understood and transformed into computer programs, and this forces a higher system specificity. Data and procedures become 'harder' and more precise.

The combinations of these generic characteristics provide the technical capabilities of IT in data handling and in communication and also condition the diffusion and usage of the technologies. In the following section the issue of IT applications in management processes and systems is considered.

Management processes and systems

Organizational processes

As was argued earlier, within any organization a large number of processes are ongoing, relating to people, data, artefacts and money. A threefold classification of such processes is used here.

PHYSICAL PROCESSES

In these, physical energy is expended in changing or moving physical entities, as in machining or assembly on the shop floor. Originally all work was of this kind, requiring human muscle power and energy or animal power, for instance in agriculture, mining and manufacturing. Historically, the whole focus of developments of tools and machines, and later, automation, has been in this arena, and not surprisingly the bulk of the literature on technology and labour process is about physical work (discussed in a previous section). While technological applications were patently changing labour process, and thus issues of labour control, there were also consequences for management.

In Bright's (1958) studies, as process uncertainty or ambiguity was reduced, there was a movement toward integrating equipment, standardizing operations and production sequence changes, all management issues. Ford combined the idea of interchangeable parts and line assembly, according to Abernathy and Townsend (1975) both concepts of process organization. Numerous changes in management practices resulted.

It would be too facile to deduce that the technologies of *mechanization* produced only peripheral effects for managers' work, for the literature documents important process changes in which managers must have had a central interest. Nevertheless, there is little in the literature which records such mechanization as changing the nature of managers' work. Mechanization, without electronic controls (before, say, 1960) was characterized by its relative lack of coupling with associated processes. In contradistinction, systems with computer controls (flexible-manufacturing systems, and computer-integrated-manufacturing) are closely coupled, not only with associated physical processes, but with the 'intelligence' system of the organization (Gerwin and Tarondeau, 1981; Boddy and Buchanan, 1982).

INTELLIGENCE PROCESSES

The word 'intelligence' is used here in the sense common to the military, implying data capture, formatting, analysis, transmission, display and associated decision making. By and large, these data processes are intended to create effective task linkage in relation to delivering products and services to the world external to the organization. Before, say, 1900 these processes would have been essentially paper–manual (PM) arrangements varying in degree and extent of specification and formality. The more specified and formalized data, and data procedures, have been commonly termed the management information systems (MIS), though according to Davis (1974), there is no agreement on the name or its exact subject area. Some intelligence processes, for instance accounting records, have been formalized and systematized for decades, and were the earliest to be dealt with by machine, firstly using punched cards, and more recently using computers (Aaron, 1969). On the other hand, some intelligence processes are highly unstructured, difficult to specify, informal and transmitted by text or orally. In general, the structure and specification of intelligence processes is highest at the lowest organizational levels and decreases as the hierarchy is ascended.

INTERPERSONAL PROCESSES

Transactions between people involve complex social, psychological and spiritual issues, and are the subject of an immense literature ranging from considerations of the personality (Maslow, 1945; Eysenck, 1965) to interpersonal and group activities (Hertzberg, 1966; Argyle, 1967; Schein, 1969). Interpersonal transactions naturally are dealing with information, and part of this may be contributing to the unstructured intelligence processes mentioned above. In addition there are interpersonal processes within difficult-to-define transactions such as motivation, negotiation, counselling, and consultation which may not specifically be involved in intelligence activities. In essence, the interpersonal processes are intended to create the most effective human climate in relation to organizational objectives.

These three sets of processes (physical, intelligence and interpersonal) are interwoven to form the total system which is the organization. The work within these processes is divided between people and machines, while the total work of people is divided among manual workers; non-manual, non-management personnel and managers (Doubleday *et al.*, 1983). However, definitions of, and boundaries between, these roles are uncertain, and as the research in this book will show, becoming more so.

Information Technology is entering:

1. The management-information-system (MIS) part of intelligence processes;
2. Intelligence processes associated with machine-accomplished physical processes, for instance systems on the shop floor. This is control engineering; and
3. Communications between people (which is a component of interpersonal processes).

While extensions of IT into these three activities will have implications for all people in organizations, consideration here is focused on the effects on the work and roles of managers. An attempt to convey these ideas pictorially is shown in Figure 2.7. Menzies (1981 and 1982) distinguishes between 'information workers', who are involved in routine entry, storage and transmission of information, for instance, secretaries,

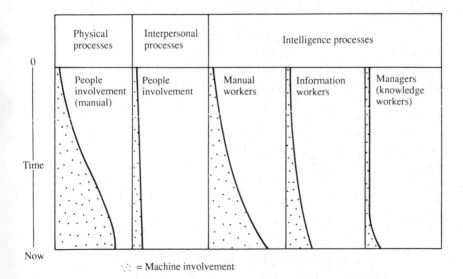

Figure 2.7 Physical, interpersonal and intelligence processes

typists and clerks, and 'knowledge workers'—the managers and professionals—who utilize and analyse information. A similar distinction is drawn by Wynne (1983) between those who relate passively to information (he terms these 'administrators') and those who perform, create, act on or with information—often the managers. Until recently the main import of office automation has been to facilitate current office-based operations, and thus influences have been mainly on information workers. According to Long (1984) a new phase of IT applications is beginning which will directly influence knowledge workers. There is a parallel here with the application of automation on the (manufacturing) shop floor which for thirty years mainly affected manual workers, but is now having direct effects on supervisors and managers (Dawson and McLoughlin, 1984; Bessant, 1983).

Managers' work

The jobs of managers are combinations of intelligence and interpersonal processes, and there are many relevant studies (Carlson, 1951; Dalton, 1959; Hemphill, 1960; Sayles, 1964; Stewart, 1967 and 1976; Campbell *et al.*, 1970; Mintzberg, 1973; Yukl and Nemeroff, 1979). Stewart sums up the situation:

We still know very little, as many writers have pointed out, about managerial work in practice. The main lesson that can be drawn from the various studies . . . is that management is a much less tidy, less organised, and less easily defined activity than that traditionally presented by management writers, or in job descriptions.

Daniel (1985), after looking at many studies, pronounces: 'little agreement on a standard taxonomy of management behaviour'. Most of the literature emphasizes the methodological problems of studying managerial work, and this is taken up later in chapter three, on method.

Rosemary Stewart's seminal works demonstrated the variability of management activity, contingent as it is on a host of influences. Fragmentation, fleeting personal contacts, lack of routines, attention switching were identified as common characteristics though the demands of particular jobs in terms of relationships, work patterns, uncertainties, exposure (the extent to which mistakes could be associated with an individual) and demands on private life were the main focus in her later text (1976).

In similar studies of managerial work, McCall *et al.* (1977) found that managers work long hours; have busy, fragmented, jobs containing much variety and brief episodes; that the work is predominantly oral; that information is the core of the job; and that managers do not have an accurate picture of how they spend their time.

The work by Mintzberg (1973) is still regarded as one of the best treatments of managerial work. Mintzberg deduces a number of characteristics of management activity:

- Much work at unrelenting pace;
- Activity characterized by brevity, variety and fragmentation;
- Preference for live action;
- Attraction to verbal media;
- The manager operates in a network of communication and contacts.

He suggests that managers use ten roles:

1. *The interpersonal roles—*
   As figurehead, ie acting as a symbol of authority;
   As leader, ie using charismatic or hierarchical power;
   As liaison, ie maintaining a web of relationships.
2. *The informational roles—*
   As monitor—continually seeking information;
   As disseminator, ie sending information from outside his unit into and around his unit;
   As spokesman, ie transmitting information out of his unit.
3. *The decision roles—*
   As entrepreneur, ie acting as initiator and designer of controlled change;
   As disturbance handler ie dealing with involuntary situations and change;
   As resource allocator, ie overseeing the system by which resources are allocated;
   As negotiator, ie acting in non-routine negotiations with individuals or other units.

According to Mintzberg, then, managers move from role to role contingent upon situations, in a more or less reactive manner at the operational level. But he hints that although to observers, managers' work seems highly unstructured, there may be higher-order 'mental programmes' limiting and controlling decision making, prioritization and so on. Mintzberg, as Stewart, is interested in:

- the character of managers' work
- 'interpersonal roles'—people issues
- 'informational roles', and
- 'decisional roles'.

And these themes occur repeatedly in the literature, though the treatment is diverse. As described earlier, interpersonal and intelligence *processes* are highly interwoven, both involve information and both are set within the cultural and structural context. The manager is thus embedded within two contiguous, and continually interacting sets of processes, each of which can be regarded as a system:

the people—interpersonal system, and
the intelligence system.

Gorry and Scott Morton (1971) used a similar approach, while Simon (1965) and other authors have been concerned with the degree of specification in intelligence processes, especially in decision making. Both these systems are dynamic and responsive to a host of forces, one of which is the 'field effect' of information technology. Deriving from the Mintzberg and Stewart traditions, and incorporating the 'system' themes of Beer, Miller and Rice, and Galbraith, a fourfold framework is adopted for the field work in the material presented in chapter four as follows:

- The character of managers' work;
- Managers and people—interpersonal roles;
- Managers and communication—informational roles, and
- Managers and decision making—decision roles.

This choice of framework is further discussed in chapter three on research method.

IT and the 'intelligence' system

IT is having most impact within the intelligence system and therefore that is discussed here in more detail. Head (1967) classifies management information systems (MIS) by level in the hierarchy (and this classification is used in the case study descriptions):

Level 1: MIS for *strategic and policy* planning and decision making.
Level 2: MIS for *tactical* planning and decision making.
Level 3: MIS for *operational* planning, decision making and control.
Level 4: *Transaction processing* and enquiry response.

To an extent this follows Anthony (1965) who suggested three types of decisions:

- Strategic planning—the process of deciding on objectives and means of their achievement;
- Managerial—control decisions ensuring efficient and effective resource use;
- Operational—control decisions ensuring efficient and effective completion of tasks.

Davis (1974) uses this format in relation to typical 'functions' of organizations (see Figure 2.8). Each function has a characteristic quantity and

FUNCTIONS

SYSTEMS ACTIVITIES	Marketing	Production	Logistics	Personnel	Finance & Accounting	Information Processing	Top Management
1. Strategic planning							
2. Management control							
3. Operational control							
4. Transaction processing							

Figure 2.8 Functions and systems activities
Source: Davis, 1974, p. 215

quality of systems activities which condition the development of IT use in that function.

All intelligence processes, including decision making, were originally paper–manual and increasingly are being influenced by IT. There are a number of 'stage' hypotheses describing the various types of IT diffusion (see for example Gibson and Nolan (1974); Nolan (1979); Meyer (1982); Hirshheim (1983)). The key aspect of these hypotheses is that organizations take time to learn about and adjust to new technologies, and they go through various stages, at different rates in office technology, computing and telecommunication applications. Thus a mix of technologies in various stages of development and usage can be found in any organization (McFarlan and McKenney, 1983). Each organization can be considered to be on its unique IT 'trajectory' according to Nolan (1979) divided into six phases. Computers, he claims, are first used on large-volume, highly repetitive, highly defined, low-complexity tasks using a single, discrete, isolated machine with limited data entry and retrieval, mostly Level 4 in Figure 2.8. Electronic data processing (EDP) is then applied serially to decreasing volume, increasing complexity, less easily defined tasks moving up the hierarchy (though there has been inconclusive testing of Nolan's stages by Lucas and Sutton, 1977; and by Drury, 1983). Nevertheless, as will be illustrated from the cases later, the exact pattern of applications of IT and the pace of implementation is unique for each organization and contingent upon the culture and management emphasis.

Nolan suggests that at first the principal force acting to introduce IT into PM processes is *cost saving*, usually implying reduced labour cost. In general, low-complexity processes (Levels 3 and 4 above) typified by payroll, order processing and accounts payable were performed by large numbers of relatively unskilled office-based personnel, and thus the potential for cost saving was large. However, as the organization is traversed upward, intelligence processes become more complex, less specifiable, less repetitive and any particular processes are performed by relatively small numbers of people, often managers. Thus the scope for cost savings decreases, and the orientation turns towards potential *value-generation*; that is to gain some competitive advantage (other than reducing cost). Hedberg (1980) suggests that in the earlier cost-savings phase, existing PM arrangements were replaced with no intention of changing the organization. Impacts were largely unforeseen, often dysfunctional and surprised both designers and users. Later, systems were more carefully designed to avoid organizational change. It is only at a third stage that systems designers attempt to use the technology to shape an organization's structure so as to increase effectiveness, and most British organizations were (according to Hedberg) not yet in that stage in 1980. Land in Piercy (ed.) (1984) concludes that even in companies with thirty years' experience of computers, there was no evidence that system designers or users looked beyond more efficient operation of the units in question. He agrees therefore that companies had not entered Hedberg's stage 3.

As will emerge later from analysis of the case studies, the implementation and effects of IT in companies are extremely difficult to classify. Nolan's 'cost saving' and 'value generation' phases, and Hedberg's reference to degree and logic of systems planning can only be regarded as useful guiding concepts. Nevertheless, entry of IT into control systems associated with shop-floor operations, and into office-based transaction processing (Level 4 of Figure 2.8) does produce effects on structure and culture and thus on the work of managers. The cost saving, and thus productivity-increasing phase, has certainly reduced numbers of personnel in the cases studied with resulting implications for the personnel roles of individual managers and for the overall personnel functions of the organizations.

In studying information systems Galbraith (1973) couples the *uncertainty* of tasks and the *amount* of information transaction needed during task execution. He defines uncertainty as the difference between the amounts of information required to perform the task and the amounts of information possessed by segments of the organization relevant to that task. He suggests that organizational forms are actually variations in the strategy of organizations to deal with uncertainty. According to Galbraith the simplest way of coordinating independent tasks is by specification of activities/behaviour in advance of the execution by rules, codes or programmes. But obviously coding or programming can only be used in predictable situations, and this becomes the limiting factor, as argued by March and Simon (1958). Galbraith suggests that there is a dynamic trade-off among five solutions to deal with the unpredictability and the overloading of management channels of communication and information handling. The five possible solutions are:

- increasing delegation, which calls for increasing the professional competence and authority of lower-level personnel;
- investment in information systems;
- creation of lateral communication paths;
- creation of self-contained tasks;
- sustaining slack resources, that is resources above the actual need for the task.

IT is fundamental to at least two of these solutions, the second and third. These several aspects of managers' work and the influences of IT on them are brought together in the next section.

The implications framework

Deriving from this analysis of the literature on management processes and systems, a simple framework was developed for research of possible interactions of IT and managers' work and roles, and is presented here. The literature makes clear that managers, a prime sub-set of the organizational system, are carrying out key work and roles, of which information processing and communications are central. Although information technology is often hyped by the hardware and software suppliers, it is certainly offering increasingly powerful, fast, accessible and low-cost facilities for central managerial functions.

In practice, as has been argued above, managers are dealing with a complex interweave of many elements. Indeed this is one reason for the expressed continuing difficulties in studying and analysing managers' work. Researchers have commonly resorted to narrowing their attention to specific components of that work such as decision making (Cyert and March, 1963; Heller, 1971); problem solving (Kempner and Tregoe, 1965); leadership (Fiedler, 1967; Adair, 1968) and ideologies (Anthony, 1986) and valuable material and insights have emerged.

Invariably, however, difficulties are encountered in isolating and focusing on separate managerial activities. It seems no mutually exclu-

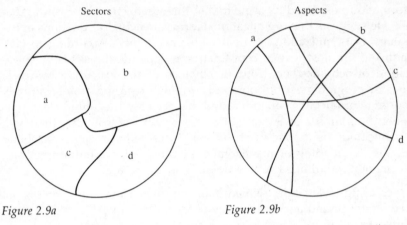

Figure 2.9a   Figure 2.9b

Figure 2.9   Aspects of managers' work

sive elements exist; each conditions and flows into the others. There is, nevertheless, a broad consensus that people, communication, information and decision making are crucial. In addition, there has been, and continues to be, considerable interest in the 'general character' of the work, for instance degree of fragmentation, brevity of episodes, attention switching and oral communication (Carlson, 1951; Stewart, 1967; Mintzberg, 1973; McCall *et al.*, 1977). These traditions are followed in this book in choosing four 'operational' dimensions of managers' work:

- the character of the managers' work;
- managers and people;
- managers and communications; and
- managers and decision making.

These do not represent separate, mutually exclusive work, roles or functions as might be described by the four *sectors* in Figure 2.9a, but are four *aspects*—indivisible, interactive and simultaneously occurring, perhaps better illustrated by Figure 2.9b. Within these four broad dimensions of managers' work there are many features which contribute to its overall character, and some of these features, for instance 'boundary issues', may be relevant to more than one dimension. In fact, in the same way that these operational dimensions are interactive and indivisible, the *features* are likewise: they are equally difficult to separate and identify. The classification shown below and used later, in the casestudy descriptions and analysis, are therefore arbitrary, but have been chosen to offer a realistic and practical view of managers' work.

The characteristics of IT (discussed earlier) which may be influencing managers' work are considered to be:

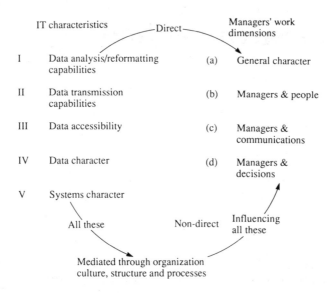

Figure 2.10   The implications framework

- Data analysis/informatting capabilities;
- Data transmission capabilities;
- Data accessibility;
- Data character (timeliness, comprehensibility, relevance);
- Systems character.

However, as with the four operational dimensions of managers' work, the effects of these IT characteristics are also difficult to separate and identify. Some influences of IT on managers' work may be direct and local while others may be mediated through organizational culture or structure, or through non-management processes. An example of this mediation is the changes in the 'people' aspects of a manager's role brought about by reduction in numbers of staff and the changes in staff skills, both associated with automation, and often at locations distant from that manager.

Although it was impossible to treat the above five IT characteristics as discrete features, the simple framework above (Figure 2.10) was used to structure the method and fieldwork undertaken in this research.

3 Research method

There are neither good nor bad methods, but only methods that are more or less effective under particular circumstances in reaching objectives on the way to a distant goal. [Homans, 1949]

The methodological debate

That research has contributed hugely to human progress needs no emphasis, nor that method has been the subject of vast debate. Even in relatively tightly bounded research areas where experimentation can be well defined and repeatable, there are doubts about method. Nobel Prize physicist Polykarp Kusch has stated: 'There is no scientific method and what is called by that name can be outlined for only quite simple problems.' Indeed even in this realm of physics, universally regarded as using highly objective and rigorous methodology, great problems exist both in acquiring valid data and in its interpretation. As Bohr (1934) puts it: 'An independent reality in the ordinary physical sense can be ascribed neither to the phenomena nor to the agencies of observation.' To quote Brightman, another Nobel Prize physicist: 'There is no scientific method as such but the vital feature of the scientists' procedure has been merely to do his utmost with his mind, *no hands barred.'*

It is no surprise that in the social sciences, where the canvas is replete with open-ended issues, and where the political, social and psychological objectivity of the observer can never be unbiased, there has been continuous, and often acrimonious, debate about method. 'At any given moment, of course, "social science" consists of what recognized social scientists are doing—but all of them are by no means doing the same thing, in fact not even the same sort of thing. Social science is also what social scientists of the past have done—but different students choose to construct and to recall different traditions in their disciplines' as Wright-

Mills (1959) puts it, in offering his 'each his own methodologist' theme. He suggests that the correct methodological and theoretical approach cannot be known in advance: it is necessary to develop 'imagination', and a sense of craft, to interpret the factual significance of the theories, and the theoretical significance of the facts.

Homans (1949) advises a similar approach: 'People who write about methodology often forget that it is a matter of strategy, not of morals. There are neither good nor bad methods, but only methods that are more or less effective under particular circumstances in reaching objectives on the way to a distant goal.' Smith (1975) further stresses the need for 'methodological imagination'. That sociological research in practice is very different from the descriptions found in (even classic) text books is commonly illustrated in the literature (see Gouldner, 1967; Platt, 1976; Bell and Newby, 1977). In his *Enter Plato*, Gouldner discusses 'method versus methodology' and warns that it is easy for reason to become 'methodolatorous'—'compulsively preoccupied with a method of knowing, which it exalts ritualistically and quite apart from a serious appraisal of its success in producing knowledge'.

Much of this realistic writing on doing social research advises a pragmatic approach, taking advantage of the situations offered and using such methods as will yield some contribution to the research process. This is, of course, not to say that the individual methods should be prosecuted with anything less than the highest rigour. What is being recommended (Webb *et al.*, 1967) is a 'multiple operationalism, a collection of methods combined to avoid sharing weaknesses'. Denzin (1970) calls this 'triangulation', and Bessant (1979) suggests that 'multiple methods can take a variety of forms: using insider and outsider perspectives, long and short term studies, operating simultaneously at different levels and locations, using historical and current data sources etc'. This is the basis, he says, of a 'contingency methodology' where choice of technique can be related to the research situation.

Studying managers

Studying managers appears to be especially difficult for their jobs are set within the complex political, social and psychological context of an organization needing a deep experience of that organization to be aware of, let alone understand. Further, as described in chapter two, all the evidence is that managers' work is composed of brief, fragmented, fast-moving episodes, and that orality is prime—all difficult to observe, to recall, to document and to analyse. Researching the work of managers inevitably follows the general traditions of social science methods, namely use of documents, observation, interviews and questionnaires of various kinds and in various combinations. Published and unpublished documents such as correspondence provide indispensable data, particularly in understanding the history of an organization. 'Pas de documents, pas d'histoire' of Langlois and Seignobos in 1898, is still true.

Material published by companies is slanted toward the anticipated readership, which may be customers in the case of sales literature, employees for internal journals or shareholders and the public at large for annual reports. While each of these sets of documentation in the cases to follow yielded useful data, awareness of possible 'halos' was critical. According to the Webbs (1932) the most satisfactory type of documents are those technically known as 'records', which they define as 'intended to convey instructions regarding a transaction, or to aid the memory of the persons involved in the transaction'. But with our current understanding of the complexity of organizations even these documents are suspect. However, for the organizations to be described later in this study, records of financial accounts, of numbers of people employed and of organizational structures were used and appeared to have good reliability when checked against interview material.

Personal diaries are a reputable source of data according to the literature ('We are safe in saying personal life-records . . . constitute the perfect type of sociological material' (Thomas and Znaniecki, 1919); 'Autobiography is the highest and most instructive form in which the understanding of life comes before us' (Hodges, 1944). But personal diaries are rather different from the self-observation and self-recording used extensively by Carlson (1951) and Stewart (1967). The latter are often limited by the pressure of management time to two to four weeks' duration and require a strong discipline that cannot be sustained easily over long periods given the fragmented nature of managers' work. In my experience, over many years of using self-recording methods, managers have much greater difficulties in using diaries than has been claimed in the literature. Other systems of self-study and self-recording, such as 'job behaviour episodes' (Dubin and Spray, 1964; O'Neill and Kubany, 1959) have been used, but suffer similar drawbacks to diaries: responsibility for accuracy and continuity lies with the participant.

Homans (1949) suggests that 'some social scientists will do any mad thing rather than study men at first hand in their natural surroundings'. While there is wide acknowledgement of the necessity and efficacy of direct observation, there are also many dilemmas in its utilization, and controversies in its utility. Firstly, there is the longstanding argument about the effect of the observer on the observed (already referred to in the realm of physics). Unobtrusive measures such as the anthropological method, in which the observer lives within the culture, remaining 'invisible', are a powerful tool (Sayles, 1964; Bell and Roberts, 1964). But here researchers must understand and interpret their observations often without the benefit of cross-referencing (triangulation), must support their findings by anecdote rather than more systematic methods and cannot replicate their work. Nevertheless, undoubtedly the insights into specific, and usually narrow, slices of society, or of an organization, which have derived from this method are invaluable, for instance in the classic *Men Who Manage* by Dalton (1959).

In contrast, obtrusive measures are now recognized as having intervention effects on the observed situation. In the 'Hawthorne' studies these effects became overwhelming; the fact of being observed became enormously more important to the workers than the experimental physical changes being studied (Urwick and Brech, 1947). Again, such methods have been often and usefully used. The greatest disadvantage of observation lies in the amounts of researcher time involved and the narrow sample which often results. Because of my familiarity with all five companies before and during the field work there is a degree of observation, albeit relatively minor, in my work here.

As Madge (1978) has it: 'The interview—and its half-brother, the questionnaire—is popularly regarded as the method par excellence of social science.' After all, as social scientists are interested in people, if they want to discover something about a person, surely the best way is to ask him or her. It turns out, as with all methods in the social sciences, that it is not that easy—there are several dimensions along which the interview varies. An important scale is that of richness versus precision—how to choose between an approach providing richness of material and an approach offering confirmable exactitude. Cohen and Taylor in 'Talking about Prison Blues' (in Bell and Newby (eds), 1977) describe their initial rambling informality, hoping that saturation would eventually allow useful themes and dimensions of experience to surface. It became clear that their notes resisted such structuring: 'The range of topics was too great, the levels of analysis too varied, the differences within even so apparently homogeneous a group were impossible to comprehend.' Accordingly these researchers moved toward a somewhat more structured approach.

The degree of structure is again a sensitive subject. It is now widely accepted that the interviewee is strongly cued by the definitions of the field inherent in the questions and for that matter the various subtle, and not so subtle, ways in which the researcher emphasizes certain parameters. (See, for example, Rosenthal and Rosnow, 1970.) There is also the associated problem of having a frame of reference which has utility to the research, and also makes sense to the interviewees. As Steven Smith writes in his unpublished doctoral thesis (1985): 'It was not that the questions were inappropriate, rather that my respondent did not describe his work in the order I had expected.' Smith abandoned his questions and adopted a 'prompt list' which proved, for him, a satisfactory solution. McCall *et al.* (1977) argue that the most serious problem in studying managers is the development of descriptively accurate, unambiguous and comprehensive categories for classifying activities and suggest that this will always be elusive. As Zweig (1948) points out: 'You must aleady know quite a lot before you can put the right kind of questions in the right way.'

The use of questionnaires has received much attention, particularly in recent years during which public opinion surveys on nearly everything are considered essential. As with interviews a central problem is what to ask and how. Hodgson *et al.* (1965): 'To construct questionnaires, we had to know the salient dimensions of the situation we were studying. It took a year of field work to find them out, and by that time we were already obtaining so much data that questionnaires would have been of no "incremental value".'

Reading the literature's catalogue of difficulties of obtaining and understanding data in the social science field, and particularly in studying managers, confirms the immense problem posed in learning almost anything of value which is reliable. Mintzberg (1973) examines, and criticizes, all the methods: although it seems the simplest way of finding out what managers do is to ask them, the results, he says, are disappointing. 'To ask a manager what he does is to make him the researcher—he is expected to translate complex reality into meaningful abstraction.' Mintzberg considers there is no evidence that managers can do this effectively: in fact, there is ample evidence that managers are poor estimators of their own activities. In spite of these difficulties, all the methods continue to be used, and continue to yield useful data.

Method for this research

In this work because of the author's long-term knowledge of the companies and the relative ease of access which this would allow, and the time available, it was decided to use a combination of interviews and the collection of published (including newspaper articles on aspects of the companies) and unpublished material. After 90 per cent of the interviews were completed it was decided to add a questionnaire procedure to gather certain data and to extend the survey beyond the interviewed group. In addition, as mentioned earlier, company visits were used to observe managers and non-managers going about their tasks.

A schema of the three major components of organizations, and their possible interactions with IT, was created at the outset, guided by the original research questions introduced at the end of chapter one, and the literature studies.

- Structural components—numbers of staff, numbers of kinds of staff, hierarchical tiers, functional demarcations, structural complexity.
- Process components—data movements, decision making, data ownership, communication, planning and control, time horizons.

- Management culture components—attitudes regarding technology, effectiveness, training, visibility and priority of strategy, etc.

From this schema and drawing on the literature and on personal experience, a set of hypotheses were created, and these follow:

Structural relevance
(1) The number of people reporting to any manager is decreasing.
(2) The proportion of professionals and skilled people in the subordinate group is increasing.

Process relevance
(3) The responsibility of any manager for data and for artefacts is increasing.
(4) The technical, ie related to machines, data and systems, components of any manager's role is increasing.
(5) Managers are increasingly using electronic data and message handling.
(6) Managerial actvities concerned with integration and function boundary crossing are increasing.
(7) There is a diminution in the manager's greater access to data relative to permitted access of other role-holders.
(8) The data-progress-chasing activities of managers are increasing.
(9) Planning is increasing and controlling is decreasing in the roles of managers.
(10) IT is producing local effects and concommitant effects distant from points of application.
(11) The IT system is carrying out increasingly higher 'intelligence' organizational processes previously carried out by people.
(12) Organizational specificity in terms of data, timing and systems is increasing.

Culture relevance
(13) The difference between management and non-management roles in terms of access is decreasing.
(14) Management roles are becoming more team-like and less hierarchical.
(15) Organizational roles in general are becoming less routinized and call for more initiative taking, and that management roles are becoming less definable in terms of routines.
(16) Managers' apparent activity rate is decreasing and reflective activities are increasing.
(17) As IT permeates an organization all roles gain more managerial activities, and the distinction between management and non-management roles decreases.

From the schema, and these hypotheses, a set of interview questions was derived and discussed with several researchers working in the field, and who all advised using a semi-structured approach. The questions were therefore composed in that format, and piloted with six managers (see Format 2 at Appendix 2). It was immediately apparent that the questions were inhibiting flow from managers, and following the comments of Smith (1985) mentioned earlier, a more open form of the questions was formulated (see Format 3 at Appendix 2), as well as 'prompt lists'. With experience, the order of the questions was re-shuffled to allow the interviewee to convey his own emphasis, and priorities, to the subjects discussed, as the interview proceeded. This approach felt more real and usually, but not always, produced a stream of relevant, useful and reliable data. Usually managers welcomed the opportunity to explore their roles, and often the problem lay in closing the interview, rather than in getting the process going. My thirty years' experience of management, and at least fifteen years' knowledge of each of the investigated companies, were considered to be of major importance in obtaining reliable and valuable data in interviews which naturally depended on credibility in terms of management understanding. I had made at least ten visits to the plant and offices of each company over these years, had observed factory and office processes and had detailed discussions with many managers. The field work interviews took place between July 1984 and January 1986. Use of a tape recorder was considered but rejected because of its possible inhibiting character.

A simple five-tone format was chosen for the questionnaire, which took twenty to thirty minutes to complete. Drawing upon the interview material (then virtually complete), managers were asked to compare their present activities with those five years previously. The questionnaire was appraised by four post-graduate researchers, amended and piloted with a group of middle managers with whom subsequent discussions were held on understandability of the questions and again amended.

Part of the questionnaire was designed to allow classification of managers into groups:

A   —specialist IT manager (for instance, management information services, computer department or an exclusively IT-orientated role in a functional department—such as a computer program manager in an engineering department).

B/C—'More IT involved' manager (considerable use of IT equipment, software, and involvement in systems design or modification). It was originally intended to separate managers in the 'middle-ground' into a greater (B) and a lesser (C) degree of IT involvement. However, this proved impossible. The indicator B/C is therefore used in the text as a reminder of the range and variety of this group.

D —'Less IT involved manager' (little use of IT equipment or software and little involvement in systems design or modification). Managers in this category were easily identified.

The discrimination into these categories was based on:

- Whether visual display unit (VDU) in own office.
- Whether personal computer (PC) in own office.
- Number of computer packages used per day.
- Number of hours per week spent on systems design or modification.
- Number of minutes per day 'hands on terminal'.
- Number of electronic messages per day.

Choice of companies

In parallel with consideration of method, defining which organizations and which managers should be interviewed, was proceeding.

To reduce the variety of organizational culture the decision was taken to select a single organizational grouping. The following were considered:

- The National Health Service
- Local government
- Manufacturing companies
- Retail companies
- The gas industry

A strengths–weaknesses–opportunities–threats (SWOT) analysis in relation to the research was carried out for each of these groupings, and from this, manufacturing was selected for these reasons:

1. the author had a strong background in manufacturing over twenty-five years;
2. manufacturing was likely to include many, or even all, facets of IT applications (that is shop floor robotics, office computing and telecommunication); and
3. manufacturing in the United Kingdom was considered to be in decline and employment nationally was below 20 per cent of employed population at the time of writing. There was likely to be interest in IT effects on the health of the industry by government, the Manpower Services Commission (as was), the Confederation of British Industry, etc.

Next, twelve potential companies were identified and tentative enquiries made via senior managers. Five of these, all of which were well known to the author, were chosen to give a range of situations, and work began. It quickly became clear from the richness of material being uncovered in these companies that they would be an adequate study in themselves. For example, their variety revealed strong differences related to specific organizational cultures.

The companies all requested anonymity, and throughout the following pseudonyms were used:

Case A   Engineering   mechanical engineering products
Case B   Hardwear
Case C   Fashion   women's clothes
Case D   Integral   electronics
Case E   Components

The sample of managers

Because the intention was to discover organization-wide effects of IT, it was decided to study a cross-section of managers, in several functions and at several hierarchical levels. In each case access for the research was given willingly and a high degree of cooperation was forthcoming. Naturally the circumstances and organizational configuration of each company was different and the exact pattern of interviews and returned questionnaires depended on many factors—primarily characters of people and departments, but also the then current economic, social and political climates. The prime objective of the research was always uppermost, and whatever opportunities came were taken to gather data. What emerged were unique cases of five sets of managers, each set operating within a highly specific culture of many dimensions. Each set was different also in the hierarchical, functional and geographical mix of managers, though in every case several functions were represented, and the range of authority was from senior executive (director level) to junior management. (Definitions of 'level' were specific to each company: 'junior manager' to one could have meant 'supervisor' to another.) As will be seen, the material revealed varied substantially, so that although a basic parallelism of presentation is used in chapter four, emphasis is somewhat different in each case.

The research included study of a particular slice of each company, namely:

Engineering —one site (11,000 employees), whole company except manufacturing and technical functions. Company was part of a giant multi-national; (30 interviewees).
Hardwear   —one site (1,100 employees), all functions on that site. Company was part of large multi-national; (21 interviewees).
Fashion   —three sites (800 employees), but mainly on two sites. Mostly production and distribution functions; (11 interviewees).

Integral — two sites (1,200 employees), but mainly on one site (450 employees), all functions represented on that site. Company part of large British national (19 interviewees).

Components — one site (2,300 employees), all functions. Company part of large multi-national (17 interviewees).

From the schema introduced earlier, a data base was constructed having the following elements:

1. Manager's knowledge of IT
2. Managers's skills re IT
3. Manager's attitudes towards IT
4. Current involvement of managers in IT
5. Vertical tiers (hierarchy)
6. Number of managers
7. Number of professionals
8. Organizational mode/complexity of structure
9. Functional demarcation/integration
10. Systematization of functions
11. Relations between this unit and rest of company
12. Centralization/decentralization
13. Rapidity of data movement
14. Decision making
15. How well informed central/senior managers are about in-house matters, particularly of operational levels
16. Data bases creation/use
17. Ownership of data
18. Automation of procedures
19. Human intervention in processes—'progress chasing'
20. Organizational flexibility/rigidity
21. IT strategy
22. Reasons for IT applications
23. Sources of push for IT applications
24. Post-event analysis of applications
25. Balance of responsibility of manager for people, data, expenditure, physicals
26. Communication patterns
27. Balance of initiative taking/conforming
28. Degree of specialization
29. Time scales
30. Boundary crossing
31. Role systematization/specificity
32. Balance of planning/control
33. Balance of informal behaviour/systematized procedures
34. Conflict
35. Changes in knowledge, skills, attitudes for management effectiveness (due to IT)

36. Manager's feelings about degree of preparation (for IT)
37. Future training/education/development needs of managers

The material from each interview was reformatted into this thirty-seven-element data base, company by company. Thus, eventually all comments of managers regarding a particular element were brought together. The system provided identification of comments by the function and hierarchical level of managers. A precis of each interview script was made, and key issues raised by each manager were entered into an analysis sheet.

From the data base and analysis sheets, and from the questionnaire results, the material was recast for each company into the four themes introduced at the end of chapter two, and incorporated in the 'Implications Framework', namely:

- General character of managers' work;
- People issues;
- Communications;
- Decision making.

A draft of the description and analysis was submitted to a senior executive in each company and either written or oral comments received. In one case ('fashion') a comprehensive discussion on the material took place with the personnel director. At 'Components' a seminar based on the draft was conducted with eight senior managers, including the personnel director. The complete material was also presented, and discussed with, a group of forty managers, not from the subject companies, in eight ninety-minute sessions. The final drafts benefit from these sets of consultations.

The total method can be summarized thus:

1. Semi-structured interviews were conducted with 101 managers, ranging from directors to junior managers, in several organizational functions, in the five companies. These interviews were the principal source of research data in this book.
2. Five-tone rapidly completable questionnaire survey used among the interviewed managers, and managers not interviewed, in the companies. Although a five-tone scale was used for answers to questionnaires, only three tones (higher, same, lower) are actually quoted, as it was felt the discrimination by managers over five tones was unlikely to be realistic. Caution was exercised throughout in interpreting questionnaire results, bearing in mind 'halo' effects.
3. Collection and study of published material (company reports and product brochures), and unpublished reports, statistics and notes. Relevant newspaper articles were also used.
4. Observation of managers, and non-managers on forty-nine visits to the companies.

5. A detailed questionnaire was completed by the manager responsible for computing in each company which gave historical technical data in the acquisition and use of IT in that company. (This manager was also interviewed in depth.)
6. Drafts were submitted to, and discussed with, key managers in each company. Oral presentations were made to a group of middle managers (not in case companies).

Interview and questionnaire forms are in Appendices 2 and 4.

Thus the research can be characterized as 'action orientated', with the method developing dynamically from the revealed data, in the style of Bessant's contingency methodology mentioned earlier.

Format of the case presentations

In chapter four, each company is analysed and reported separately. Within each company analysis, organization functions are, where possible, dealt with in the following order:

Generic function	Typical departments
● Finance	accounting, costing
● Technical	design, development, draughting, technical writing
● Manufacturing	production, quality control
● Supply	purchasing, inventory control
● Marketing	sales, public relations, advertising
● Systems	management information systems (MIS), data processing
● Personnel	personnel, training

The generic function names (underlined above) are used in each company to give a standard framework, though names of functions, and of departments within functions, differed between the companies and sometimes within a company. Department names are used where they aid clarity.

Within each function, wherever relevant, descriptions and quotations are given in the tier order of managers, with highest tier first, that is:

● Chairman or Managing Director
● Directors
● Senior executives
● Middle managers
● Junior managers

For each company the order of sections is:

- The company
- Information technology implementation
- The character of managers' work
- Managers and people
- Managers and communication
- Managers and decision making
- Summary of IT effects (for that company)

It would have been possible to describe and discuss the fieldwork under the headings above, combining material from the five cases. However, the prime issue under study is the work of managers, with all the cultural and structural conditioning, of a specific company. To preserve this cultural integrity, the material is presented as five distinct cases.

The research is primarily a survey of IT effects on managers in five companies, and conclusions presented in the final chapter (five) are drawn from the complete width of the material. However, some comparisons and contrasts between companies are presented in the summaries at the end of each case.

The order of presentation has been considered carefully: Engineering comes first because it has had a long history of IT implementation and manifests a rich variety of implications. Hardwear is second, partly because it, too, is an engineering company, and partly because it is also well developed in IT usage. Fashion comes third because it is the least 'IT developed', is in a completely different field and so offers contrast. The two electronic companies come last, for evidently they are quite different, from each other and from the other companies. Components completes the set, for it may give the best guide to the future of IT and managers.

4 Information technology and managers in five manufacturing companies —the case studies

Our first mistake was regarding the computer as a glorified accounting machine. [Director—Engineering]

IT helps me run my business better. We deliberately have a high spread and availability of PCs and terminals—to do a lot more analysis than we used to. The skill is to use the data well . . . [General manager—Components]

In this chapter, the fieldwork material from the five companies is presented in the following order: (1) Engineering; (2) Hardwear; (3) Fashion; (4) Integral; (5) Components. Each case begins with the IT culture in that company, and the extent and kind of IT applications already implemented, under way and planned. The influences of IT on the four principal dimensions of managers' work, developed in chapter two as 'the implications framework' are then presented. Summaries of IT effects conclude each section with brief comments comparing and contrasting that company with others previously described. In the thesis resulting from the research there is extensive direct quotation from managers. Much of this has been eliminated here to give a more compact account, though it is hoped that the meanings have been retained.

The format for each case is: (1) the company; (2) IT implementation; (3) the character of managers' work; (4) managers and people; (5) managers and communication; (6) managers and decision making; (7) summary of IT effects. To maintain anonymity all identifying characteristics of the companies have been deleted.

Case A—Engineering

The company

Engineering is a very large British subsidiary of an American multi-national designing, manufacturing and marketing complex consumer products. Its history is of slow growth for the first twenty years (in the early part of this century) and then acceleration in growth until in 1971 37,000 people were employed. In the years since, the labour force has fallen and stood at around 20,000 at the time of the research. Since the early 1970s the company has faced intense competition and this has forced a deep re-evaluation of all dimensions of its operation, not least its products. Traumatic organizational restructuring characterized the 1980s. Nevertheless, at the time of the study, there was cautious optimism about the current greater customer acceptance of products.

Thirty people were interviewed, all at the largest factory site, four directors, nine senior managers and seventeen middle and junior managers. These managers were in finance (seven), marketing (seven), purchasing (seven), personnel (four) and management information services (five). Twenty-two of these managers filled in the questionnaire. The company requested that questionnaires should only be distributed to the interviewed group.

IT implementation

It seems that neither Engineering, nor its parent corporation, had seen IT as a major issue for management in the years immediately before the study. The corporation's policy of delegated autonomy to constituent companies meant that IT in its may forms was developing in the group without overall coordination or standards for hardware, software or systems. At Engineering, use of computers and information systems had been evolving for more than two decades, in the early years without a company-wide overview. More recently developments were guided by a management information systems committee, not surprisingly chaired by the financial director—for MIS lay within the finance function. This committee set tactical priorities but did not appear to include telecommunications or automation in its perview. Nor were implications of the technologies—for instance management structure or training—much considered. IT it seems, was visualized principally in terms of replacing existing paper–manual (PM) systems with more effective computer-driven versions—with the intention of reducing head-count. In fact, reducing head-count is a major issue, heavily promulgated from the parent corporation in the United States, but widely seen by managers at Engineering as counterproductive. IT was thus presented as a short-term cost-reduction opportunity. This is in line with the 'cost-saving' orientation claimed by Nolan (1979) to precede an 'added value' orientation toward IT.

The average length of service among the interviewees was twenty-eight years—many managers had been in the same department, and often in the same role for several years. Organizational charts were quoted often, as were the well-understood levels of authority, remuneration and perquisites. In fact, the ambience was the most 'bureaucratic' of the five companies. In addition managers saw their jobs as relatively secure, and expressed caution and even apprehension about the innovations which IT might bring. Paradoxically, a widely voiced belief was that Engineering was lagging behind its competitors in its adoption of new technologies. On this risk-aversive, strongly structured culture, systems based on the main-frame computer had been impinging for years with limited enthusiasms among managers. However, at the time of the study, personal computers were being introduced and were finding favour. Whereas user-managers often thought main-frame systems were restrictive, difficult to understand, inflexible, their comments about PCs were the reverse. The personal computer was seen generally, but not always, as an immediate adjunct to their own management processes, totally under their own control and 'friendly'.

In spite of the relative neutrality of senior managers to IT, it was clear that corporate moves were afoot to give a greater strategic importance to the new technologies. Interconnectability standards, especially for manufacturing automation equipment, were receiving attention; a joint venture with a leading Japanese high-tech company was in being; a data processing company was purchased and was taking responsibility for MIS throughout the corporation.

IT IN THE FUNCTIONS

The finance department had a long history of machine data processing—from punched-card onwards. However, managers in the function do not seem to have been overly enthusiastic about computing. Indeed it was a commonly expressed opinion among non-financial managers that the location of management information services within finance was a mistake. Nevertheless, there had been twenty-five years of continuous development of machine systems—first into 'transaction processing' (level 3 of Head, 1967)—payroll, accounts payable, receivables, general ledger and later into operational control (level 4 of Head). At the time of the research several highly sophisticated systems were being designed and introduced.

Although a computer system was brought into the supply function in 1967 it seems there had been numerous obstacles to its implementation—not least a generalized lack of understanding of systems—according to a senior executive. Highly expert specialists, analysing and designing systems and powerful hardware, were frustrated by this lack of systems knowledge and skills among managers in general. Once again in this function there was evidently an acceleration in systems applications over the last year or two partly stimulated by the introduction of PCs.

It was in marketing that a much higher level of enthusiasm towards IT was found among managers who were convinced about the 'added value' to be gained from the technology. The analytical power of computers in relation to market data, and the speed and responsiveness of systems networks were widely appreciated. It seemed in this function that a new 'milieu' was emerging with small teams of enthusiasts creatively generating new approaches—in contrast to the rather conservative and reluctant acceptance of systems commonly found elsewhere.

There had been almost no use of computer systems in the personnel function until very recently so there were few observable direct effects of IT. However, managers in the function were well aware of the potential for change inherent in the technology and commented widely on staff reduction and skill changes. It was not possible to arrange interviews with managers in the manufacturing and technical functions. In technical, sophisticated systems for design, specifications and planning were in place, while manufacturing was regarded as tardy in take-up of new technologies. Thus the extent of computer developments varied—indeed not only was each function and level of management different, but each manager had a unique story to tell.

The character of managers' work

As will unfold, every company was involved in changes of all kinds, many but of course not all related to technology. Managers were therefore much involved in, and concerned about, the management of change. Within the rather conservative ambience at Engineering, change, especially rapid and technologically-based change, was regarded with apprehension. Managers were often faced with direct involvement in designing or establishing a new computer system, and in managing the accompanying structural, process and social alterations—usually without sufficient training themselves either in the technological aspects or in 'organizational development'.

All the interviewed managers at Engineering were primarily involved in 'intelligence', that is data gathering, analysis and dissemination, although much of this was still conventional paper–manual. Main-frame systems had existed for twenty years or more—so much computer data was available. Managers tended to say that their roles and activities had been little changed by this well-established main-frame environment. On the contrary it seemed that it is the impact of the new wave of IT— the rapid spreading of the technologies, the personal computer and the greater emphasis on systems which is forcing change on managers.

It is important to emphasize the variation in IT involvement among

	A	B/C	D
VDU in office per manager	.7	.1	0
PC in office per manager	1.0	.2	.1
Number of packages used daily	3.2	2.1	.4
Hours per week on systems issues	13.3	12.1	1.1
Minutes per day on terminal or PC	137.5	18.4	0
Electronic messages sent per day	5.5	.2	.2

Figure 4.1 IT involvement of managers (from questionnaires)

managers. Three categories of manager were identified: 'A' managers are specialists in some aspect of IT, for instance in MIS or as a computer 'expert' in a functional department such as marketing. 'B/C' managers are 'more-IT-involved' (but by no means computer experts) as deduced by an analysis of their apparent use of hardware or software or involvement in IT-based systems. (The dual letters are a reminder of the wide range of involvement of this group of managers.) 'D' managers are 'less IT-involved' and often not involved at all. Although this classification is used for all five companies, its use is primarily to identify differences *within* each company. Thus comparisons of, say, 'B/C' managers between companies must be carefully handled (see Figure 4.1).

As mentioned earlier, each manager's story regarding IT was unique. It was clear, however, that the technologies had little direct impingement on the highest-level executives. Except for the financial director who was chairing the IT overview committee, other senior people expressed little interest in the issues or implications. It was at middle-management levels that direct impacts of IT were most apparent, where the main battlefield lay, where the tensions between the new and the old were being worked out.

The perceptions of most interviewed managers were that the pace of their work had increased over recent years, though there was no apparent differentiation between IT-involved and IT-less-involved people. Observation suggested that IT-involved managers were extremely busy—perhaps because they usually were managing the existing work arrangements, while trying to introduce a new computer-based system. As the local culture was usually at best conservative, and often resistant to the changes, managers expressed frustration, especially as they felt they were getting little support from the top.

The characterizations of managers' work in the literature (for instance Stewart, 1967 and 1976; Mintzberg, 1973; and McCall, 1977) were confirmed. The managers at Engineering were busy, switching their attention frequently, and with high fragmentation of work. Managers appeared to be involved in many tasks simultaneously, interruptions were common and a key skill seemed to be assessing priorities of urgency and importance. The introduction of IT appeared to further reduce any existing routines and formality in managers' jobs while increasing codification and specification of processes which were being managed. Data specificity, timing, formats, routing and authorization to access data all became more disciplined. It is important to differentiate the effects of IT in terms of specificity on tasks (often data transactions), on staff and on managers. As IT moves into a section, tasks become more codified, staff jobs are influenced differentially, but managers' work becomes even less prescribed.

There is a sense in which all activities of a manager can be categorized as dealing with the present or preparing for the future. It is tidy in concept to see planning as a distinct undertaking as per Fayol (1916), but in practice the time dimension of managers' moves from the present to the future, and to the past, instantaneously and often. In interviews managers had enormous difficulty in disentangling these time threads. Formal planning could be easily identified, but informal planning is thoroughly interwoven in the fabric and its emphasis and extent in the role of individuals was difficult for them to assess. But managers at Engineering did believe they were giving more time and emphasis to planning in recent years. Although this is impossible to ascribe entirely to effects of IT there was a feeling among the more involved IT managers that the added data disciplines were forcing longer time horizons on them. Here again the paradoxical nature of IT implications was evident. The rapid response characteristics of IT tended to increase the focus on the immediate, while simultaneously the fast data access and analysis allowed managers to speculate about the future with the sophistication only possible with 'what if' packages on their personal computers.

Managers and people

Although at the time of the survey the labour force stood at less than half its historic maximum of 37,000, it is still a big company. Not surprisingly 'people issues' had been, and still are, overwhelmingly important. Matters of remuneration, conditions of employment, health and safety, general personal administration and the associated trade union interest in all these absorbed a great deal of managers' time and focus. Personnel and industrial relations departments were well established and busy. Patently, the people dimension of most managers' jobs is large and important. The question was: how was this changing as IT impinged on managers' roles?

NUMBERS OF PEOPLE

The evidence throughout the company was that numbers of people at all levels had been reducing for years, but especially since 1980. Headcount receives continuous and heavy emphasis. Naturally, staff reductions are brought about by several simultaneous mechanisms so interwoven that it was impossible to prove unequivocal linkage between IT and staff reductions. There was always a complicating feature: titles of jobs and of departments, and the company's structure, had been changed often over recent years and this was happening as a wave of 'newer' IT was being applied. Even managers local to a particular application had difficulties quoting personnel numbers.

In addition, post-event analysis of IT applications were rarely made, at least in an exact and formal manner. There was then, no apparent accumulation of analytical evidence within the company which categorically demonstrated a specific staff reduction associated with a particular scheme. Nevertheless, managers often gave anecdotes of direct staff reductions as an IT scheme came into use. They also pointed out that besides the discrete labour loss resulting from the introduction of a new system, there was a steady erosion of labour as the many aspects of IT favourable to effectiveness altered the total data-handling culture. This is dealt with later under managers and communication.

SKILLS OF PEOPLE

No data were taken in this research of the views of subordinates of their own skills and activities. But managers' perceptions of the skills and activities of their subordinates were discussed at length with managers.

Apart from hand–eye coordination skills in jobs like typing, the competencies used in clerical-administrative-professional jobs are indeed difficult to define, identify and understand. What was clear throughout this research was that most managers are unable to be specific about such skills. Needed skills, knowledge and attitudes were talked about in an undifferentiated way. The perceptions of managers were that as IT usage increased, the skills and competencies needed by subordinates were different, and usually 'higher' or more 'sophisticated'.

A typical high-IT-usage section was in marketing. Here virtually every member of the team had a degree; there were no clerks. Everyone was intimately involved in computer systems—calling up data from several networks and using sophisticated analytical packages with a high level of creativity and initiative taking. The picture was of an enthusiastic, organic team with profuse one-to-one transactions between them and a low hierarchical profile. Managers of such groups (there were several) used words like 'flexibility, 'responsive', 'initiative taking', 'creativity', 'enthusiastic', 'high calibre', 'analytical'. The contrast with conventional paper–manual sections was stark. Clerical and even lower-management roles there were repetitive, staid—in fact the virtual antithesis of a high-IT section. Once again the paradoxes were evident. With increasing IT the dimensions of data—format, timing, routing—become more prescriptive, but the active roles of data users may become less prescriptive. In groups highly involved with computer systems, there was an increasing tendency for staff to know about systems and data from outside their functional boundaries. Further, there was a pressure from such systems for rapid response—and this catalysed people to act more swiftly—for instance in inputting data, or in decision making. Because of these two elements (knowledge across boundaries and response speed) it appeared that clerical staff and junior managers were more likely to deal with exceptions themselves. In fact, in such sections the skills of juniors became more like those of their managers.

MANAGEMENT OF PEOPLE

Organization charts were much in evidence at Engineering, and managers talked, almost without exception, about their position in the hierarchy. Status and authority levels were delineated relatively obviously, as were reporting lines and responsibilities. Role rotation was not a tradition; in fact most managers had been in the same function for many (tens of) years. This long role incumbency implied reinforcement of functional boundaries and conventions. The overwhelming impression was that people-management had a strong flavour of gaining compliance among subordinates to a well-established and relatively 'bureaucratic' set of expectations. Initiatives had generally not been encouraged. The sheer numbers of people, many in low-level clerical and manual work, meant that the 'personnel administration' within managers' jobs—issues about time-keeping, absenteeism, grievances, hour-by-hour communications, detailed queries on activities—had to take priority.

As paper–manual jobs decreased, replaced by IT, the number of clerical–manual roles has been steadily reducing and the skills required have been increasing. Coupled with this was a growing independence of staff, in terms of obtaining data and using it, and in their being required to take initiatives which previously would have needed management guidance. Managers were therefore wrestling with their own changing roles: their authority deriving from hierarchical designation was ebbing. On the other hand, team building and the associated participative skills were needed, as were leadership roles in understanding and using the computer systems. While the management training department appeared to have an understanding of these tensions and their resolution, by and large managers were coping with these complex cultural and skill changes as best they could with little training.

Managers and communication

As discussed in chapter one managers are intrinsically pivotal in the 'intelligence' and interpersonal processes of organizations. These two aspects of communication are inextricably interwoven yet they are different. The intelligence processes are essentially focused on creating the most effective task linkage in relation to delivering products and services to the world external to the organization. On the other hand, interpersonal processes are concerned with the continuous maintenance of the optimum human climate in relation to organizational goals. But naturally some of each of these is contained within the other.

STRUCTURAL ISSUES

Organizational structure gives one view of the character of communication. Was the increasing use of IT altering structure at Engineering? Historically the company had been very large, somewhat mechanistic, bureaucratic and, in the best sense, a paternalistic organization, with strong functional and departmental boundaries. Reporting and communications appeared to be relatively disciplined. Organizational charts were much in evidence (and considerably more so than in the other four companies): managers had a high expectation of 'knowing where they were'. Traditionally there had been many organizational layers with clear 'tier' positions in terms of status and authority. Organizational coordinates of managers in terms of both function and hierarchy were thus widely known, and there was a corresponding clarity of responsibilities, reporting patterns, linkages and roles. (Of course, in all these descriptions it is necessary to continually presume the word 'relatively', for each manager's role is unique.) However, because of the sheer size of the company, the many constituent departments and sections within them, and the reporting patterns to corporate layers above the company unit, the structure at Engineering must be described as complex, yet traditional.

Departments tended to be quasi-autonomous, with inhibited boundary-crossing, both in day-to-day exchanges and in the movement of personnel between roles in different functions. Because managers were a part of this culture, as would be expected, often they would be unaware of the degree of 'bureaucracy' as compared with other organizations. Nevertheless, it was quite common to hear anxiety from managers about the rigidity of boundaries, the lack of role rotation, the watertightness of functions and departments. Also, especially from managers who had experienced other companies, there was often concern about 'staidness' and lack of initiative-taking.

While it would be wrong to ascribe powerful structural change forces to IT, it was clear that several aspects of structure were being influenced as computer-driven systems spread and were becoming an inherent and important aspect of the company. Although paper–manual systems prior to IT were interconnected between functions and departments, those interconnections were less specific than computer systems demand. IT forces specificity of data formats, routing, timing, procedures— and this forces and allows 'correspondence' of data across boundaries. This in turn pushes integration and coherence of functions.

It is worth repeating here that the *indirect* effects of IT are at least as important and powerful as the direct effects, and often these indirect implications are distant in time and space from the point of the IT application. Also these indirect consequences may interact with each other making interpretation difficult. For instance, as mentioned earlier, the labour force at Engineering had been falling for years—certainly partly due to applications of technology—and numbers of managers were reducing also. The numbers of subordinates reporting to the first-line supervisors of the managers had fallen slightly (and approximately in line with similar falls in three other companies studied) and the falls were greater where IT was more prevalent. But a separate and often ruefully quoted effect of IT systems was increased organizational transparency. 'Top executives can now more easily monitor what is happening at operational levels . . . the "bull" doesn't cover up so much' (E-7).

Managers consistently reported a reduction in tiers in the company and occasionally were able to show that a specific management layer had gone entirely. This is consistent with the two IT effects mentioned above, reduction of people and greater transparency. Another effect was increased transparency in the other direction—that is subordinates had greater access to data. This was a marked perception of most interviewed managers. Thus although definitive structural changes due directly to IT were impossible to pin down, there was a strong awareness among managers that system coherence, integration and organizational transparency were increasing, while 'designatory' definition—for instance functional boundaries—was weakening.

DATA ISSUES

The 'information management' component of managers' roles was plainly increasing. Involvement in data gathering, analysis and dissemination was widely and consistently perceived as more time consuming and important. Generally managers claimed increased comprehend-ability of data, though this was tempered by frustration about the amounts of data, and often the amounts of paper, produced by computers. Once again there were two themes in opposition: computers gave too much paper, yet the available data was easier to understand and was more useful. (Certainly if the paperless office is coming it was a long way off at Engineering.)

In two ways, IT systems presented increased speed of data effects. Patently, electronic data processing is essentially lightning fast. Once the definition of what was required, its format and the access formula were understood, then undoubtedly managers were impressed with the increased speed with which they could get at and analyse data. But there was a second effect. As IT systems linked functions and departments, and as data formats became more coherent, the mechanisms and behaviour inhibiting data transfer across boundaries were becoming less powerful. The specificity of data ownership was decreasing.

Electronic mail was little used: mean number of messages sent daily by the surveyed group of managers was five, and only 25 per cent of them had the facility. Of course these two things go together. In fact, most IT systems were used in 'operational' settings, and the screens were used mostly by clerical staff and not directly by managers. Most managers were not trained in the use of terminals—and were equivocal as to whether they wanted to develop such skills.

ORAL COMMUNICATION

In line with the vast research evidence on managers' work, oral communication remained dominant at Engineering. Managers reckoned that they were actually spending more time talking with their immediate subordinates than previously. Consultation with more senior managers was also seen as increased. While both of these perceptions might have been wishful thinking, there was no evidence at Engineering that oral communication was decreasing in amount or in import as computer systems became more used.

As managers were adamant that they spent more time on data and systems matters—*and* that there was more consultation with both superiors and subordinates, it is an interesting, but unanswered question as to what elements of their jobs a few years earlier were now *not* being done.

Managers and decision making

The interwoven nature of managerial work stressed in chapter two was especially apparent in the arena of decisions. At Engineering, and as will be seen later, in the other four companies, managers had the greatest difficulty in defining and explaining their involvement in decision making. While 'people issues' and 'communication' had a certain substantiality, decisions were more ephemeral, if minor, or blurred by consultations and committees, if major. Further, information processes and decision processes were always entwined: the same IT factors influenced both. It was frequently mentioned that initiative-taking received little encouragement—the culture emphasized sticking to the rules. Although computing had been spreading within the company for two decades and was now an inherent factor in the decision apparatus, it seems to have largely merged with the existing conservative culture. Managers commonly perceived this main-frame computing as having slight effects on their practices. This was further confirmation of the power of cultures to perpetuate themselves in spite of an apparently perturbating force such as computing.

The recent developments of IT and its diffusion are of a different nature to main-frame computing and its effects. The several generic characteristics of the technologies (discussed in chapter two)—speed, universality and especially the personal involvement in, and control of, systems—do appear to be altering decision practices. As data bases and systems become more integrated, the inhibiting nature of arbitrary functional and department boundaries becomes less. Not infrequently managers commented on this increased integration: data transactions across boundaries were built into the systems and required parallel consultation between managers in the separate departments. The impression was gained that the degree of consultation on decisions was thus being enhanced.

Similarly, senior executives were automatically presented with information derived from operational levels almost in real time. This continuous monitoring was not lost on the lower- and middle-order managers. On the other hand the speed of data transactions produced a pressure on managers (and on others) to respond quickly, to take decisions faster. Here then was a cadre of managers cultivated to be rather cautious, now being pressed by systems to be more responsive, and yet knowing that their decisions, or at least the consequences thereof, were being monitored pretty acutely from above. An interesting formula.

Another dimension is the reduction of routine personnel administration in operational departments as numbers of staff fall as a result of computerization. Associated with this is an apparent lessening of the 'monitoring of staff' role of managers as professionalism and sophistication of subordinates increases. As was suggested earlier it seems that as the use of IT increases, the differences between management and non-management roles become fewer. Another effect is that some decisions are being absorbed into the machine-system itself or are vanishing as system designs are enhanced. Thus IT appears to be softening boundaries, increasing pace, responsiveness and transparency all related to decision making—and in this company all dissonant with the existing culture.

Summary of IT effects

At the outset it is important to emphasize the great variety in IT applications at Engineering in mode, extent and sophistication. In some departments a third-generation system was being used by staff highly experienced in the technology. In others IT is entirely novel. Thus, although it is possible to derive some conclusions about IT effects on the whole organization, it is clear that the technology cannot be regarded as being uniform either in application or in its implications. IT has many characteristics and these interact with the composite of structural, cultural and process elements at various coordinates in the organization. At Engineering the total culture is undergoing a significant transition in relation to IT, though outcomes vary from manager to manager and must always be regarded as transitional.

There has been no revolution. Rather, newer, more effective, more integrated, faster systems have been evolving and replacing previous paper-based arrangements or computer systems of an earlier marque. Again, while that statement is a general truth, some subsequent systems turned out to be worse, or more confusing, or less effective than previous arrangements and have been abandoned or modified. In some instances, it was difficult to convince the designer IT specialists that their creation was indeed less than perfect, and this situation produced frustration at the operational levels as managers and their staff struggled to make sense of the new system.

The principal source of system design, and motivation for IT implementation, lay with the experts in management information services (MIS). Priorities for applications were set by the MIS committee chaired by the finance director and from their viewpoint there was a strategic plan. However, most user–managers perceived the spread of the technology to be tactical—and indeed as the prices of hardware continued to fall, and as PCs became more available, it did appear that tactical forces were gaining ground. Though here again, because Engineering now has a sister company entirely responsible for MIS, the overall approach to IT has probably become more professional. User–designer tensions, discussed by Friedman (1983) were plainly evident, perhaps more especially because in this company the speed of developments of IT and its fluidity are dissonant with the prevailing culture and practices.

The parent corporation seems to have given little weight to the technology before 1980. Since then there has been an accelerating increase in corporate attention to robotics, automation and systems. But the historic momentum, accumulated over decades, is powerful—the cultural preparation of managers for new ideas, systems and equipment must be regarded as slight.

Computer applications had been diffusing for more than twenty years and at the time of this study over one hundred programs or systems were in place. In the way Nolan (1979) has described, applications initially were in high-volume, simple transactions such as the payroll, but have gradually extended into more complex, less high-volume activities in most functions. So, at an organizational scale, managers have had a slowly expanding exposure to computer practices—though it must be remembered that each incremental system's step was a discrete event for the managers concerned. In the last three or four years IT has quite suddenly become a major issue for many managers at relatively the same time as terminals, personal computers and word processors became widely available. With this greater availability came the beginning of the transition from Nolan's 'cost saving' phase to his 'added value' phase. Managers apparently began to appreciate the IT advantages of timeliness, clarity, accessibility and speed of transmission. Virtually all managers claimed their involvement in, and knowledge of, computers and systems had increased substantially over recent years.

As IT enters a department staff numbers decrease, while the proportion of skilled and professional people increases. Hierarchical and functional structures tend to become less constraining—data and managers becoming more able to cross boundaries. Integration between departments tends to be improved and the total number of sub-systems to fall. Managers often said they had a broader, less parochial view of company affairs—an advantage in their eyes.

The implications for managers' roles are neither clear-cut nor easily identifiable. Certainly managers are spending more time on systems analysis, design and management than previously. About a quarter of the group had a terminal or personal computer in their own offices— though the average usage was only sixteen minutes per day. Electronic mail was used hardly at all. It is important to distinguish between IT effects on systems and effects on roles. For instance, there appears to be a tightening of disciplines in terms of data formats, routing and timing, coupled with improved data clarity and reporting procedures. Increased access to data and to 'packages' for data analysis were generally welcomed by managers. On the other hand, managers commonly expressed uncertainties as organizational transparency increased and as their specific ownership of data decreased.

Subordinate staff also are gaining increased access to data—and, because of pressures of rapid response inherent within the strengthening IT culture, are often called upon to engage in 'management-like' skills—initiative-taking, flexibility and information analysis. Where high levels of IT are used, highly professional groups are developing with team building and team management skills supplanting the traditional, hierarchical management styles.

For managers there seems to be a trend away from routine, repetitive 'personnel administration' and people-monitoring roles. Managers still see themselves as devoting much of their time to people issues but in a less formal way. They thought their time frames were longer, that strategic matters were receiving more of their attention. Undoubtedly IT has now become an important influence on culture, structure and processes at Engineering and especially on the roles and work of managers. But the picture is complex and full of paradoxes.

Case B—Hardwear

The company

Hardwear is the British manufacturing and marketing unit of a large international company in a highly competitive precision engineering field. Launched in 1910 the company expanded in output, number of employees and product range to a peak in 1970, although cutbacks in demand had begun to appear in the mid-1960s. The period from 1976 until 1983 was especially difficult with intense Japanese and other competition. Financial losses were sustained in seven out of those eight years, and two of the three manufacturing sites in the United Kingdom were closed. Rationalization of product range and a much improved distribution of production among the several manufacturing sites—in various countries—took place in the early 1980s. At the time of this study Hardwear employed 1,100 people and had an annual turnover of £70 million.

Twenty-one people were interviewed: six at director level, ten at one level below director and five at one level below that. In addition thirty-two questionnaires were returned. The researcher also spent two weeks talking informally to managers and observing them. It is worth recording here that job titles and 'tier' levels were not a sound guide to levels of responsibility and authority: this was true in all the companies. For instance, factory managers, nominally at level four at Hardwear (level 1 = MD), carried a heavy responsibility for both large amounts of capital equipment and large numbers of people, and were working in strenuous conditions. In contrast some technical managers were at an apparently higher tier level yet their managerial responsibilities seemed comparatively slight.

IT implementation

Hardwear is part of an international corporation with some eighty plants, 170 companies and 50,000 employees. There were many examples given of a strong strategic framework orchestrated from the European head office—commonly referred to as 'group'. There is (according to the MD) a written-down corporate strategy for IT covering commonality and compatibility of systems, common data bases, IT in manufacturing, scientific computing, inventory logistics, international planning and customer data links. However, no other manager claimed to have seen a written strategy for IT, and nearly half the interviewed managers thought there was no plan for information technology. As has often been observed, the concept of strategy is elastic. Here the MD was confident there was an IT strategy yet most of his managers were sure there was not.

Within Hardwear, IT strategy was claimed by most managers to be determined by the local directors in monthly meetings, yet according to two of these directors the discussion had a mostly technical orientation. Priority setting for, and checking progress of, specific systems being developed were the main topics. There was no written-down programme of intended consequences of new equipment or systems beyond the technical improvement of an operation. Implications for personnel, training or for organizational changes in terms of responsibility, authority, communication and decision making were hardly considered. With the exception of the director of information systems, no great enthusiasm for, or understanding of, IT emerged in interviews with directors. Indeed one of that group said no director was 'that interested' in the subject. Among managers who were involved in systems applications surprise was frequently expressed at the relative lack of understanding among their senior colleagues of the strategic importance of IT and at the slight effort which was being made to increase knowledge and skills of the technology in the company generally.

What emerges then is a variety of responses to tactical pressures with different emphasis and evolution of IT practices in the several functions. Interestingly, although the original company emphasis was in production and engineering, neither of these departments have been in the vanguard of IT, which at first sight might be thought of as a close relation. Nor had the finance function been much interested in extending the sophistication of their computerized systems. It is the marketing function which has the greatest enthusiasm for the technology. There, an energetic systems steering committee seemed well convinced of the sales potential of providing customers with an excellent computerized information service on prices, deliveries and technical products. To quote the marketing director: 'IT is the key to our future . . . product differences between us and our competitors are decreasing, therefore the back-up services become more important . . . and rapidity of data handling is at the centre of this.'

IT implementation had thus proceeded in a patchy fashion dependent on the knowledge, enthusiasm and vision of the senior managers in the different functions. The 'champions' of the technology had an over-whelming influence in determining pace and direction of change—at least as much, it seemed, as the formal structures and procedures. Certainly, tension between the widespread commitment to maintaining the status quo and the IT thrusters was evident. A similar story to that at Engineering.

The character of managers' work

IT INVOLVEMENT OF MANAGERS

As described in the methods chapter, the managers studied were divided into three groups: systems/computer specialists (A) of which there were four; managers implicated in IT activities (B/C) and managers little involved, or not involved, in IT-based work (D). Each of the latter two groups was about the same size in terms of questionnaires returned: eleven B/Cs, twelve Ds. Interviewed group sizes were: ten B/Cs, nine Ds. The systems specialists were entirely immersed in IT activities and issues, and they provided a rich source of data on the applications of IT and on implications for managers. The report here looks at the roles and activities of managers with particular references to the differences and commonalities discovered in the two manager groups (B/Cs and Ds).

The pattern of interviews and returned questionnaires by tier and by function is shown in Figure 4.2. The MD is regarded as Tier 1; those reporting to the MD are Tier 2. The split between B/C and D managers in the total group approximately reflected the amount of apparent involve-ment in IT in the *functions*. (Note: The average age of the B/C group was thirty-eight and for the D group forty-six.)

The B/C group were clearly aware of being in a dynamic situation. Part of this was due to the transition from paper–manual (PM), to computer-based systems; part seemed to be an intrinsic quality of IT involvement (see Figure 4.3). For B/C managers, IT had become a major focus: indeed 70 per cent of this group felt it was the source of the biggest changes in the company for years. Information gathering, analysis and dissemina-tion, and involvement in computer-driven systems, and knowledge of such systems were all claimed by these managers to have increased. The recognition that much 'office-work' is centred upon data assembly, and therefore is eminently suitable for computer-assistance, surfaced in a number of B/C interviews.

a. Tier

Tier	Questionnaires			Interviews		
	A	B/C	D	A	B/C	D
1 & 2	1	1	1	1	1	4
3	3	7	4	1	6	3
4	0	3	7	0	3	2
Totals	4	11	12	2	10	9

27 questionnaires
(15 from non-interviewed managers, 12 from interviewed managers)
Total group = 36 managers

b. Function

Function	Questionnaires				Interviews			
	Tier				Tier			
	1/2	3	4	Total	1/2	3	4	Total
MD	–	–	–	–	1	–	–	1
Finance	–	2	1	3	1	3	–	4
Technical	–	–	5	5	1	–	1	2
Manufacturing	–	2	1	3	1	3	3	7
Marketing	1	5	3	9	1	4	–	5
Systems	1	3	–	4	1	1	–	2
Personnel	1	2	–	3	–	–	–	–
Totals	3	14	10	27	6	11	4	21

c. Function

Function	Questionnaires				Interviews			
	IT involvement*							
	A	B/C	D	Total	A	B/C	D	Total
MD	–	–	–	–	–	–	–	–
Finance	–	3	–	–	–	3	1	4
Technical	–	1	4	5	–	1	1	2
Manufacturing	–	–	3	3	–	2	5	7
Marketing	–	7	2	9	–	4	1	5
Systems	4	–	–	4	2	–	–	2
Personnel	–	–	3	3	–	–	–	–
Totals	4	11	12	27	2	10	9	21

*Involvement primarily discriminated on time spent on systems issues, on direct use of terminals or personal computers, on electronic mail usage, and on apparent amount of interaction with computer produced data.

Figure 4.2 Pattern of questionnaires and interviews by tier and by function

	B/C	D
VDU in office: per manager	.4	0
Personal computer: per manager	.2	0
Number of packages used daily	1.8	.2
Hours/week on systems issues	3.1 to 5.4*	.8
Minutes/day on terminal or PC	59 to 89*	3
Electronic messages sent/day	.75	0

*Includes two managers very highly involved in IT

Figure 4.3 IT involvement of managers

The D group of managers (in all functions) saw themselves in a more stable situation—only 40 per cent of these people saw IT as a major source of change. However, even though their direct IT involvement was much lower than the B/C group, there was an evident influence of computers and IT systems upon their roles and upon their view of the organization and the future.

PACE, FRAGMENTATION AND ROUTINES

It was in the marketing function that the immediate impact of IT was most apparent. From the director down, there was a common assumption that IT was now quintessential, that it offered major competitive advantages and that it should be implemented as fast as possible. There was widespread use of computer analysis, transaction processing and electronic communications throughout the function, coupled with a feeling of *fast response, and pace.* As in the other companies, increased 'pace' is often associated with greater application of IT.

While all the studied managers appeared to have fragmented jobs, with brief activity duration, and little time for reflection, the 'IT-involved' group seemed to have fewer routines and an increase in proactivity and responsiveness. There was an impression that a linkage exists between the degree of routine paper–manual processes of their staff and the degree of routine in their roles. Managers frequently believed IT absorbed the routine department jobs and therefore tended to make their own roles more varied.

BOUNDARIES

Greater IT involvement seemed also to be associated with crossing functional boundaries. The managing director explained that technology was making the organization 'more complex . . . many blurred boundaries . . . it is only possible to locate the centre of the task . . . managers have to take a broader, more integrated view'.

There were many examples given of this increasing integration across functional boundaries—boundaries which before the introduction of sophisticated IT could be carefully guarded, but through which information could now easily and instantaneously pass. And as information becomes easier to access electronically across these boundaries so, it seems, managers inevitably must transact orally as well. One example was the extensive interconnections between manufacturing engineers and accountants as more complex IT-driven cost systems were coming into use.

PLANNING AND TIME HORIZONS

As discovered throughout this research, IT appeared often to have paradoxical implications. For instance, because IT produces useful data rapidly, and because of real time communications, it cues managers to react to present situations, and thus drives out personal and informal planning. On the other hand, IT-involved managers affirmed that their concern with strategic issues, their focal point in time ahead and the elements of (formal) planning in their job had all increased. (In contrast D managers thought these matters had stayed the same or decreased.) Part of the reason may have been that increased IT systems forced a more coherent analysis of the inter-relationships, and the time-dependency, of sub-systems on managers. For instance, it was clear that in both manufacturing and marketing, where sophisticated and integrated IT schemes were being developed, those involved took a longer, and more proactive, view of the business than the D group or even their management seniors.

Managers and people

NUMBERS OF PEOPLE

The number of people employed at Hardwear had fallen dramatically since 1975, following the international corporate rationalization of production. Without exception, managers quoted general and specific examples of this reduction. Tier 2 and tier 3 managers consistently cited diminished staffing levels, but some tier 4 managers quoted increases in the numbers of their own subordinates. This confirmed the generalization, often referred to, of a 'flatter' structure. Instances of reduced staffing brought about directly by increased technology proved difficult

	1980	1985	% Reductions (corrected for changed turnover)
Managers/Supervisors	70	42	38
Professionals	49	27	43
Skilled clerical	37	37	0
Unskilled clerical	21	16	20
Skilled manual	201	98	51
Unskilled manual	1357	453	65

Figure 4.4   Staff reduction in manufacturing function

to elicit. Plainly the amount of IT-based activity was increasing as evidenced throughout Hardwear by more terminals, computer-driven systems and print-outs, and computer telecommunications. Equally plainly there were widespread examples of greater use of technology being the cause. But other possible causes were quoted and blurred the picture, no doubt because of the sensitivity of the jobs—technology relationship. Managers throughout the company commonly spoke of anticipated further reduced staffing, usually among unskilled, semi-skilled and professionally unqualified personnel. Staff reduction in manufacturing is shown in Figure 4.4. Although some of this reduction could be attributed to product rationalization and to the eradication of overstaffing, a proportion was due to increased automation and computer-based controls in the factories.

D (less 'IT-involved') managers claimed, on average, that the number of their subordinates was the same as five years ago; the B/C ('more IT-

	Numbers of staff reporting directly to manager			Numbers of staff manager responsible for (not directly)		
Tier	Mean	Most common range*	Range	Mean	Most common range*	Range
2	6.3	3–9	3–9	162	10–100	10–675
3	3.2	2–5	0–8	55	10–20	0–600
4	3.3	0–6	0–11	17	1–6	0–150
Overall	3.4	3–6	0–11			

Note: Occasionally professionals with a 'management' title had no staff reporting to them.
*80 per cent or more of managers in this range

Figure 4.5   Numbers of staff responsible to managers

involved') group perceived a small fall, while computer specialists reported a 25 per cent fall in their own staff. As IT involvement increased so did the tendency to report staff reduction. Generally the reports were of a greater reduction in the lower-skilled people, manual and clerical, so that the proportion of professionally qualified and skilled personnel had increased.

In Hardwear the altered functional boundaries, plus the movement of managers—usually promotions—made it impossible to determine precisely the changes in personnel in any section over the last five years. However, it was possible to discover the current reporting patterns which are shown in Figure 4.5. Usually, managers studied, had between three and six people reporting directly to them and responsibility altogether for two to twenty subordinates. By far the largest numbers reporting to managers were in the manufacturing area.

SKILLS OF PEOPLE

Although specific figures on reduced staff could not be obtained, many managers believed that staff numbers were reducing and that subordinates were becoming more technically aware and skilled. Indeed there was constant reference by managers to a higher calibre of employee, both in qualifications and in terms of professionalism and 'brightness'. Also many interviewed managers emphasized the greater need for training—and not only in IT-specific areas. 'Increased flexibility' and 'initiative taking' were also often mentioned by managers as needed skills in subordinates, a picture which often emerged in this research.

MANAGEMENT OF PEOPLE

Although reduction in overall staff numbers was patent, managers consistently reported their time on 'people issues' had increased over the last five years—and this was especially so among the 'IT-involved' managers. The 'management of people' roles and style of the studied managers had little detectable consistency. Certainly no manager quoted any company principles, policy or strategy regarding personnel. Nor was there a clear division of managers into 'old-schoolers and new-schoolers'. Most managers had been with the company many years (commonly more than ten) and the differences of view about staff management appeared to be functionally orientated. As the spread and intensity of use of IT was itself functionally differentiated, management 'style' and behaviour, in relation to people were (again) associated with IT involvement. This overlaps with communication issues discussed later, but marketing and systems managers tended to speak in team rather than in hierarchical terms of their subordinates. The 'small business team' concept was being developed in marketing, with 'as much discretion as possible at the salesman level'.

In manufacturing, where control of machines and quality control had been installed, but where IT data systems were relatively unsophisticated, there was also a trend in the same direction. Thus although IT was evidently implicated in staff reduction, and in the need for teams, it seems there are other forces at work tending in the same direction.

Training was a continuing theme, both for the managers, and for their staff. Undoubtedly managers thought the diffusion of IT-based systems was being retarded by lack of management skills, imagination and appreciation of the potential of the technology. One executive was still surprised at how senior managers did not understand the strategic importance of IT and did little to improve their understanding. However, a project was under way to improve management and technical competence throughout the company. Even so there was anxiety that insufficient training was taking place. H-18 (manufacturing): 'I am not happy about the level of knowledge and skills my staff have— insufficient attention is being paid to training . . . and into manpower implications [of IT].' A senior executive in manufacturing said: 'It is difficult to recruit foremen for sophisticated (production) lines. One of the mistakes I have made is not having sufficient education and training for managers and supervisors—especially technological training.'

Managers and communication

All the managers studied at Hardwear universally perceived themselves as heavily involved in information gathering, analysis and dissemination.

STRUCTURAL ISSUES

As in Engineering, there was almost unanimous comment about the ease of boundary-crossing, and an increase in organizational transparency, both across functions, and vertically, brought about by IT. The managing director especially emphasized this increased organizational integration and the consequent requirement for managers 'to understand the whole picture'. This illustrates another apparent characteristic of IT systems—the 'positive feed-back loop'. Holistic management is only possible because of sophisticated IT networking allowing timely data and wide accessibility. But because of the latter, holistic management becomes *necessary*.

Many comments were made about increased visibility—often associated with increased *vulnerability* of managers. Phrases such as 'the fog is less' and 'managers are more exposed' were common. H-2 (marketing) gave an example: 'There is a lot more visibility of operational levels . . . staff now chase answers because the questions are visible to senior managers . . . it is difficult to hide . . . managers are out in the open and this is changing the kind of manager who is competent.' Similarly in Finance, H-3 said: 'People still try to protect their areas but data is accessible across boundaries—middle managers are more vulnerable— their data is easily exposed.'

No structural changes could be unequivocally associated with IT, but what did emerge was a picture of boundaries, both hierarchical and functional, more traversable by information, and to an extent, by managers themselves. Increased transparency, and accessibility of data seems also to be linked with an increasing *responsiveness* of managerial and non-managerial processes. While these effects were found mostly in departments much involved in IT systems, there appeared to be similar, but slighter, effects beyond those departments.

DATA ISSUES

As discussed in the section on implementation, the numbers of termi- nals, screens and PCs, and the availability of computer-produced data has steadily increased over the years, and most managers regarded the systems–data component of their roles as large and important. Computer-produced material had usually become a standard part of the job and, apart from comments about format-unfriendliness, or about difficulties of getting a format changed, was regarded as unremarkable.

Systems had often been installed ten to fifteen years earlier (for instance costing, and inventory) and had become accepted as the 'nor- mal' hard-data infrastructure. This now traditional regime was being overtaken by the switch from batch to on-line, the spread of PCs, the telecommunication emphasis and the impending installation of much more integrated systems (for instance in manufacturing). As in the other companies, it was important to understand the *specifics* of a system and its implications, especially the particular phase of an installation. Early systems produced (and were still producing) voluminous print-outs which stimulated managers to complain of excessive quantity or irrelev- ancy, while later schemes, using on-line screen access, were much more acceptable on these issues. However, perceived increase in data quantity, and in information issues in their work, was most marked among the B/C group, as was the apparent utility of print-outs, and data timeliness.

The characteristics of IT which appeared to have the most remarked-on effects were rapidity of processing or transmission and accessibility of data, and these features are associated with the spread of the new genre of systems. Electronic mail was still rarely used by managers internally, but messaging over the international Hardwear electronic network was being used by some interviewed managers who found it very useful. But it was the spread of electronic data bases with their virtually instantaneous access and display of needed information, and the links between customers and the company via networks which were most mentioned, again mostly in the prime user area of marketing and distribution.

ORAL COMMUNICATION

Managers' roles were patently mainly oral, one-to-one and in meetings, and increased time talking to both their seniors and their subordinates was often intimated. This was especially observed in marketing, sales and distribution departments and in the production areas, where factory managers were immersed in a sea of direct personal contacts. These managers, often with more than one hundred subordinates, appeared to spend a large proportion of their time in talking to shop-floor workers and supervisors and participating in many meetings—at least one per day—on a host of diverse subjects: stock control, costs, quality, cleaning, rejects, lockers for staff, overtime, tidiness, new installations. In addition it was obvious that computer-produced data was entering their work in a substantial way, and one of their problems was coping with the transition as the detailed people issues decreased and the computer data issues increased. While this was true of all interviewed managers, it was especially observable for factory managers and in sales administration.

Managers and decision making

On all aspects of decision making, managers at Hardwear appeared to have difficulties in defining and recalling their roles and behaviour. Decisions seemed to be so woven into the continuing stream of events, and so blurred by interactions with several people and often committees, that they were rarely remembered as distinct events. Issues were often successively refined and changed as more, and different, information became available and as understanding altered. Decision making was patently closely associated with information transactions and with interpersonal relationships.

GROUP INFLUENCE

In matters strategic, the guiding presence of 'group' was omniscient, though several managers emphasized the consultative–participative relationships with 'group'. Nevertheless, managers frequently gave the impression that they were not taking initiatives because 'group' were working on the problem. The corporation had carried out a huge (European) rationalization of product range, and of production facilities over the past five to seven years. Its consequences for Hardwear in terms of manpower reduction, closure of facilities, reduction of product range and of operations generally were never far from the surface in discussions.

As discussed previously under 'IT culture', this dominance of 'group' was immanent in the IT field. A written-down corporate 'group' strategy was said to exist, though only the MD actually claimed to have seen it, and this long-term plan conditioned Hardwear's IT local developments. For instance, Hardwear awaited the installation of an all-embracing 'group' computer-based manufacturing system and its own scheme had been abandoned in its favour. Similarly, the corporation was working on an international project (BEDA) for holding all manufacturing and technical data on file at a central location (not in the United Kingdom). Again CADCAM (computer aided design, computer aided manufacturing) was being used in other units abroad but not yet at Hardwear, although it was expected within a year.

Thus it seemed that Hardwear managers were participating in the unfolding of the 'group' IT plan. But the major IT packages were being designed abroad, with timing of implementation being much influenced by the corporation's head office.

RAPIDITY OF DATA HANDLING AND DECISIONS

Rapidity of data handling was often mentioned in the context of decision making. It was clear that in several ways information was moving much more rapidly than hitherto, and also that the handling data—that is analysis and access—was much faster than five years earlier. Message switching within the international network was now virtually instantaneous and implied a potential for near real-time consultation between 'group' and Hardwear. This facility was often mentioned, usually favourably, by senior managers and the specialists who had been using the message network. Similarly, as reported earlier, the marketing department regarded speed of data movement to and from customers, and access of data to customers, as a prime selling advantage. On the local site, there was as yet little use of electronic mail. However, much more rapid data handling (as opposed to transmission), that is data collection, analysis and access, was widely remarked upon in the context of decisions. Data base availability and usage had increased considerably over recent years and gave easier and more rapid data access when compared with older 'packages' with narrower data functionality (designed for limited tasks within, say, marketing).

The spread of personal computers was also a cause of increased speed of access and of analysis. For instance, H-15 (finance) explained that 'because of the use of PCs people are now thinking of a *complete* job, rather than splitting the task between several people'. The implication was, more speed, and a less fragmented understanding by staff.

The efects which follow from increase in speed of transmission and speed of access are subtle, and certainly not easy to identify by managers. There was a tendency of managers to imply that faster access meant better decision making, and more flexibility of organizational response. H-3 (finance) said: 'The decisional role will not change but with more up-to-date information, decisions are better. A manager knows, more quickly after a decision, whether a risk is working . . . though people do not yet understand the value of data'.

DECISION SUPPORT

Customer specification of products on receipt of customer application data was being used. Whereas before engineers would use their own experience and judgement about applications, now this knowledge had been codified into a computer package. While overseeing this process was still carried out by engineers, it was the early stage of an 'intelligent knowledge-based system'. This approach was adopted partly because of increased customer stringency on specification and price; computer-derived specifications could be more accurate and much more rapid.

In production, in warehouse assignment and in marketing the movement toward computer-assisted, or computer-guided, decision making was quoted. Every single product coming off the production line was sensed for quality and dimensional accuracy by a fully automatic computer controlled system, which fed correcting tooling data to the appropriate machines. This was a case where several tasks involving manual quality control and the associated decision making in terms of corrective measures had been integrated into a single complex computer-driven system. A similar case was in the bonus payments' system in which a computer arrangement measured and recorded product output on several production lines and calculated workers' bonus payments according to a complex set of guidelines. Here again, various previous tasks—some shop floor manual, some office-based paper transactions and some decision making—had been designed into a single IT system. As Rothwell (1984) reports, in these kinds of instances, discretionary decisions previously made by supervisors become absorbed by the computer system.

The process of decision making seemed to be less focused on specific functions, departments, tiers or even on Hardwear itself. Because of the increasingly widespread web of fast data access, traversing all functions and including 'group' and some customers, decision-making was taking on a 'network' character. Many managers talked of the necessity for a broader, less parochial management pervue and the blurring of demarcations of all kinds.

There were several differences in decision ambience between B/C managers (much involved with IT), and D managers (little IT involvement). The former felt their authority to take decisions, their emphasis on strategic *vis-à-vis* tactical issues, their time horizon and the planning elements in their role had all distinctly increased over the last five years. D managers claimed these job factors had remained the same.

Summary of IT effects

Computing had been well established in Hardwear for twenty years, yet the major part of its activities continued largely without IT interventions. Only in the last three or four years, with advances in the technology, particularly in cost reduction, personal computing, telecommunications and software engineering, has a more favourable climate for IT diffusion developed.

Although there is, it is claimed, a written-down 'group' strategy for IT, local managers are largely unaware of that plan. Nor is there apparent evidence of management considerations of organizational implications of IT; nearly half the interviewed managers believe there is no plan for IT. Implementation has, therefore, proceeded in a tactical fashion, responding to, and being limited by, the various levels of knowledge, enthusiasm and imagination among managers. There was a monthly meeting of directors on computing which dealt mostly with priority setting and checking progress of systems developments.

It was universally agreed that marketing had moved most quickly into IT-based operation and that, paradoxically, finance, in which computer involvement had started twenty years ago, had little zeal until very recently. There was unanimity also that technical and manufacturing were lagging and that the Personnel function had hardly any involvement in IT. A clear functional differentiation of IT applications and implications is therefore apparent. No revolution was seen, although there appeared to be quickening of interest in, and an acceleration of, IT involvement over the last two or three years.

A clear division of surveyed managers into an IT-involved group

(B/Cs) and a 'slightly involved' or 'uninvolved' group (Ds) is discernible. The two groups evince rather different views of management and IT issues. But a changing organizational culture associated with information technology is evident in most managers' comments, in whichever group. IT is commonly quoted as one of the major sources of change in recent years. The reduction in personnel at Hardwear (from 5,800 in 1970 to 1,100 in 1984) is mainly due to manufacturing and product rationalization and effectively blurs the labour effects of IT applications. Nevertheless, managers were able to show in several cases that increased sophistication of, and increased use of, computer systems did produce productivity gains and manpower reductions. Generally reports are of greater reduction of lower-skilled people, so that the proportion of professional and skilled personnel has increased. Managers frequently report insufficient levels of training for themselves and their staff in preparation for IT applications. Indeed, training of all types is regarded as scant.

Computer applications have been first in repetitive, 'low-intelligence' functions such as wage administration and costing. At the time of the study highly sophisticated and integrated systems were about to be introduced in manufacturing, and the expectations of managers are that these wide-scale applications will produce considerable organizational implications. Computer-driven systems are thus absorbing increasingly higher intelligence tasks, with effects on an increasingly broad spectrum of managers and functions.

As IT spreads, speed of data transmission, and data access, quickens, boundaries become less hard, and, in general, organizational transparency becomes greater. This is associated by managers with vulnerability. Coupled with this is an expressed need for integration of functions and tasks and a more inclusive management approach. The time horizon (focal point ahead) of IT-involved managers seems to be longer with more concern with strategic issues. There is widespread reference to 'changing' and 'increased' skills associated with the new technologies and among the B/C group observations of increased 'professionalism' and 'calibre' of staff. Managers consistently report they spent more time on people issues (in spite of there being less staff), though industrial relations issues are rarely reported. Oral communication remains dominant in management roles.

Communication forms a large component of all the managerial jobs, and most managers regard information transactions as a key element. Computer-produced material has usually become a routine, and often unremarked on, part of their milieu. The IT-involved group are most aware of data parameters such as quantity, timeliness and utility.

The rapidity of transmission of data, and accessibility of data, are the IT characteristics most commented on and valued. Transmission speed, and data accessibility mean more frequent interaction between managers and between managers and the data, and a gradual movement toward 'real time' management.

There is an absorption into the computer system of some data collection and sensing activities, and some decision making (for instance assignment) and evidence of some elementary intelligent-knowledge-based systems.

Decision making was difficult for managers to describe, though accessibility of data and system rapidity was thought to improve decisions. Decision mechanisms appear to be taking on a 'network' quality because of the web of IT-driven data bases and the fast consultation possible.

A COMPARATIVE NOTE

Hardwear and Engineering, although having uniquely different cultures, share many similarities. They are both foreign-owned multinationals in mechanical engineering, with long established products and have for the last ten years or so experienced vigorous competition—for which it seems they were under-prepared.

Some cultural–structural features are similar: traditional, well-defined functional demarcation and hierarchy; weakness in training and especially management training; a conservative ambience; financial losses over the last decade; little inherent experience of electronics; a twenty-year history of 'conventional' main-frame computing. On the other hand there are dissimilarities: Engineering had ten times the labour force, a much more complex organization and probably a more conservative, risk-aversive environment.

The characteristics of managers' work in the literature hold in both companies. Managers tend to have busy, highly fragmented, action-orientated work with much attention-switching and oral communication. Almost without exception the patterns of IT implementation and its effects on managers are similar. Both companies have decades of computing experience, but primarily using 'isolated' main-frames to handle transaction processing. It is in the last five years that IT has become strategically important from a corporate viewpoint, and this has coincided with the spread of terminals and personal computers among managers, and functions.

IT implementation is proceeding largely in a tactical manner with no explicit and well-known plan nor much preparatory training for managers. Each area is taking up IT in a specific way, with low-complexity, high-volume transaction processing in the finance department being the earliest user. Technical and manufacturing tended to be less IT-involved until recently, and personnel usage is slight. In both companies the marketing function has over the last two or three years become enthusiastic about the potential of IT both for decision support and for fast telecommunications. In recent years, the availability of personal computers and networking is a source of a more favourable acceptance of IT by users.

Cost reduction as productivity increases appears to have been the principal early motivation for using IT, though added value is now emerging as a new incentive. Both companies are shrinking in size (for a given turnover), partly due to technology, and structure is flattening and becoming simpler. Functional and hierarchical boundaries are becoming less inhibiting for data flow and for consultation between managers. Integration between functions is improved with managers taking a broader, longer-term view of their business. Where IT is heavily used both managers and non-managers appear to be enthused with a new sense of initiative-taking and flexibility.

In these two companies it seems that important cultural changes are being stimulated by the spread of IT. Traditional, rather mechanistic management approaches are giving way to a new ambience.

Case C—Fashion

The company

Fashion is a medium-sized British company designing, manufacturing and distributing women's outer garments. Starting from a family partnership before World War I the company has grown to a loose federation of production plants, warehouses and 'shops-within-shops', centrally co-ordinated from London. Three thousand people are now employed with production still essentially based on skilled manual labour.

Because of the informality and loose definition of responsibilities and reporting patterns, it was impossible to categorize managers in terms of specific hierarchical levels. Managers themselves appeared to have difficulty in locating their 'tier' positions, and there was often discrepancy between a manager's stated tier position, his title and the perceptions of that role by other managers. The structure was inherently 'flat' with only about three levels between the chairman and shop-floor section-foremen.

Thirteen interviews were conducted at the 'Southtown' site, the 'St Davids' computer centre, and at 'Westholt' central warehouse: questionnaires were returned from these sites and from HQ managers.

IT implementation

In every area discussed with managers three norms soon emerged: first the emphasis on day-to-day and even hour-to-hour operational tactics; second the looseness of responsibilities and reporting patterns, amounting to uncertainty in several instances, and third the optimistic and deeply engrained acceptance of the current apparently successful way of doing things.

Labour intensity in garment manufacture remains high and at the two factories visited 'traditional' sewing predominated, accomplished skilfully and flexibly by women. Each garment requires many operations—cutting, sewing buttons, pleats, pockets, collars and pressing. Throughout, the production process used low technology, with no automation or robotics, though movement of semi-finished and finished garments between sewing stations was by conveyor. Each operation had a work-study-fixed number of work-minutes used for piece work payment and in costing and planning. It was in this field that computers were focused, as it was seen by managers as the core of the production operation.

After the initial decision to purchase the computer used by the company in 1974, the subsequent development of systems had been primarily in the hands of the computer centre manager. No evidence of a company plan for IT, or even a consensus among the interviewed managers could be found. Meanwhile a completely separate unit had developed in 1978 at the 'Southtown' manufacturing plant with a different set of hardware, software and applications. This IT centre was championed by a well-informed wages clerk with the backing of the company chairman. Applications were decided on the basis of 'What we knew best' and 'getting rid of drudgery' (F-4). During its initial three or four years there was little local support for this venture, indeed it was tolerated at best. But gradually its usefulness to the plant managers was recognized.

Undoubtedly both computing centres were not welcomed by line managers, nor was there any coordination between the centres. The applications of IT were mostly in finance, warehousing, distribution and production control. Thus in this company computers were at an early state of development with no IT strategy and little, if any, coordination of applications or preparation for implications.

The character of managers' work

Fashion was based upon traditional low-technology skills and practices established over decades, managed by people with a long experience of the company, usually on the same site and in the same job. Among the interviewed group, the average length of service was fifteen years. Factory managers had tailoring backgrounds, had moved up from the shop floor and were exclusively men. The two warehouse and distribution managers had been in basically the same job for more than twenty years. The IT managers, personnel executive and general brand managers had much less experience of Fashion (averaging seven years) and more experience in other companies than the other managers.

Of the managers interviewed three were IT specialists, four were 'involved' with IT and six were only slightly implicated with IT. The distribution by function is shown in Figure 4.6. In every case the managers studied regarded IT as an increasing element in their roles, though current time on this element and its rate of change was unique to each manager. Virtually all the managers claimed much more involve-

a. IT involvement of managers

	A	B/C	D	Total
Finance			2	2
Warehousing/ distribution		2	1	3
Production/factory management		2	2	4
Personnel			1	1
Data processing	3			3
Total	3	4	6	13

b. Pattern of IT involvement by tier

	A	B/C	D	Total
Tiers 1 & 2			3	3
Tier 3	1	3	2	6
Tier 4	2	1	1	4
Total	3	4	6	13

c. Involvement in IT activities

	A	B/C	D
Has VDU in own office: per manager	0	1.0	.2
Has PC in own office: per manager	0	0	0
Number of packages used/daily	0	.6	.6
Hours/week on systems issues	10	2.8	.9
Minutes/day on terminal or PC	5	64	6
Electronic messages sent/day	0	0	0

Figure 4.6

ment with systems and computers and more knowledge of this field than five years previously. The extent of claimed increased involvement and knowledge of IT corresponded well with the current actual use of terminals and implication in systems design and modifications.

Most of the IT applications were directed at operational level (piece work control, production control, and distribution and stock control), and the major impact on managers was at middle-management level. At the upper levels there was slight direct effect: 'IT has not made any difference at all to me—the only benefit is that people are better informed. Managers reporting to me are more numerate—'people orientated' managers may be decreasing, and 'data orientated' managers may be increasing' (F-5, director).

In interviews with four directors they first commented that IT was having only marginal influences on their roles, but deeper reflection on their activities pointed to greater reliance on computer-produced information and an overall change in their use of time, and emphasis, toward issues related to data and systems.

At the lower operational levels managers were much clearer that their roles were now heavily dependent upon, and interactive with, the computer systems. At factory manager level for instance, while the bulk of management activities were continuing more or less as previously, the output from the computer, and the greater visibility of productivity and cost factors to the MD and the production co-ordinator were changing their focus. Problem areas were identified and production amendments initiated earlier; the organizational transparency was increasing.

The traditional culture at Fashion probably allowed 'slack resources' in Galbraith's (1973) terms to exist widely. Management jobs such as production scheduling in the factory and stock assignment in the warehouse had been the responsibilities of operational managers, who, with paper–manual systems, used their initiative and considerable skill to alter tasks continually in coping with varying demands of output. And these, largely tacit management skills, worked—probably because of the existence of slack resources. Even with the relatively low level of computerization, scheduling has become tighter and a greater degree of forward thinking and planning is possible. Slack resources (ie staff and machines) are either becoming redundant or are being used to increase throughput. However, tight resources (and scheduling) are contrary to the historical nature of Fashion's culture and call for more attention to planning and analysis.

All managers studied had highly fragmented jobs constantly being interrupted by telephone calls and issues of the moment. There was no evidence that IT was changing this character. At operational (and probably all) levels of management, proactivity has been widespread and necessary. Increased computerization is probably requiring a higher level of adherence to schedules and reducing the extent of proactivity on scheduling issues by low-level managers.

This is an example of changed level of decision making. The traditional fluid ongoing series of adjustments to the production schedule initiated by floor managers is being replaced by the tighter, more systematic computer schedules. The *transition factor* again is in evidence: those early, computer-produced schedules were inherently rigid, partly because of infrequent updates and partly because outputs were in hard copy. (From evidence in the more 'advanced' companies, as updating frequency increases, and line operation via VDUs replaces printed copy, a 'smoothing' of procedures is apparent.)

The general looseness of definition of roles and responsibilities implies 'soft' functional boundaries. Managers tend to have 'spheres of influence' rather than areas of command. However, each site operates as a more-or-less self-contained entity, and managers often expressed criticism of other sites. Loyalty is firmly based on 'site' rather than on function.

Nevertheless, there was evidence that some integration was beginning to emerge. It appears that as managers are becoming more knowledgeable about data handling and analysis, the potential of IT systems for addressing the longstanding and accepted scheduling problems in production and distribution, and the issue of coordination between these two functions, is surfacing within the management group. What had for decades been accepted as the extant milieu of the rag trade is being redefined as a solvable problem. Coordination *is* possible; slack resources *can* be reduced.

Managers felt the time on which they focused ahead was longer than five years ago, that planning elements in their roles were larger and that longer-term issues were given more attention. Although some of these comments might have been wishful thinking, it did appear that the traditional and frenetic activity of managers at Fashion was yielding somewhat to the increasing disciplines of computer systems.

Managers and people

NUMBERS OF PEOPLE

At two factories studied total staff had reduced from 750 to 565 over five years while the output remained the same. These reductions were almost entirely from the shop floor though some were clerical. At the central warehouse, a launch of a new and successful label manufactured abroad had substantially increased throughput of garments and required new deployment of existing staff. Thus, although three-quarters of interviewed managers reported staff reductions in their areas, it was not possible to link IT directly with staff reductions. (This was in common with the other companies.) However, there was little doubt among managers that IT had begun to cause such reductions.

SKILLS OF PEOPLE

As mentioned earlier, Fashion has a flat hierarchy—a low, wide pyramid with large numbers of manually skilled people, mostly women, on the sewing-machines and unskilled manual workers in the warehouse. No automation has been introduced in the factories, managers said, because of the difficulties intrinsic to manipulating cloth. Thus sewing and associated skills have so far been untouched by IT. Computer operation was impinging on office and management practices in warehouse and distribution control, factory production control and piecework payment procedures. From observation the few people engaged in these systems are using distinctly different skills. It was particularly noticeable that clerical staff involved in computing were less wedded to traditional practices and often advised their managers about data and systems issues.

MANAGEMENT OF PEOPLE

Factory managers historically had been recruited for their tailoring and production expertise and for their ability to supervise operatives within the informal, traditional and low-technology environment. At 'Southdown', managers quite obviously knew their operatives well, including 'births, deaths and marriages' of their families. This familial atmosphere was also apparent between the managers. Each morning all the floor managers, and often the personnel director and MD 'breakfasted' together, the conversation ranging over issues of cloth, production, payments, delays, absenteeism—the stuff of their daily round.

Because of the incentive system, based on individual jobs completed, motivation of operatives was plainly high. There was a contented atmosphere. The managers spent a great deal of their time actually on the shop floor (and this applied also to middle management) in detailed contact with the issues of quality, production of labour. As F-3 said: 'Trouble shooting and keeping the shop floor happy.' There had been no strike for thirty-six years, he claimed. While the central warehouse was patently different in terms of work content, managers there also appeared to have relaxed, informal relationships with subordinates and peers.

No managers spontaneously talked of training or of 'development' of managers of supervisors. There appeared to be a tacit and widespread assumption that training for themselves was not required—that the ongoing arrangements were the 'natural order'. In the situation of slow rate of change over many years, the only apparent training need was for operatives to be brought up to skilled performance as rapidly as possible.

In essence, then, the style of management (in relation to people) seemed not to have been much affected by IT. The slowly encroaching computer system was requiring managers to focus more on statistical information, and that meant an hour or two engrossed in print-outs, or interrogating a VDU which in turn implied less time actually on the long-established conventional roles. Further, there were early signs that systematization of scheduling was having effects on the highly decentralized authority held by managers to deal proactively with day-to-day events. It was this authority which underpinned the status of the managers in the context of a low-technology milieu, with a. loose definition of responsibility, particularly in relation to employees on the shop and warehouse floors.

Although at an early stage, increasing systematization of production planning, a tighter coordination between functions and between sites was weakening the current 'tribal chief' role of floor managers—and there was some evidence that intuitively they may understand this already.

Managers and communication

COMMUNICATION ISSUES

As in all five companies, communication was a quintessential component of managers' work at Fashion. In all functions managers were engaged continuously in communication, much of it oral and usually face to face. The morning 'breakfasts' of the floor managers and directors at 'Southtown', the ongoing chat between managers and their staff and between the managers themselves were all indicators of a traditional, low-hierarchical familiarity. It seemed that functional and hierarchical boundaries were easily traversed, as evidenced by the daily talks between the young production co-ordinator and his local directors and his weekly consultation with senior executives at the London HQ.

Managers often quoted lack of coordination, especially between production and marketing, design and production and the two independent computer centres, all evidence of a general looseness of definition of structure, responsibilities and authority. Managers also claimed to know of no strategy in the company. Because of this culture of low structural definition, it would seem oral communication was rich—and *had to be* to offer ongoing tactical coordination and control, less available through other data channels than in the other four companies studied. The content of the oral transactions seemed to be almost entirely tactical and local: for instance two of the interviewed directors said they were never involved in discussions of long-term plans. Thus computer systems were being installed within a relatively low-innovative ambience characterized also by informality, lack of structural definition and rich oral processes. It is not surprising therefore that IT had as yet made little impact on communication practices at Fashion. Managers most involved with IT systems claimed difficulties of understanding information had decreased and that access of their subordinates to data had increased. These managers were spending one or two hours each day now on computer data issues, and obviously this work was replacing their previously 'conventional' activities.

Managers and decision making

DECISION ISSUES

As has been discussed earlier, there was little long-term planning in the regime at Fashion, at least in a written-down or pronounced form. That there must have existed a set of guiding policies is self-evident for the company had an obvious internal coherence as expressed by the commonality of approach by the managers interviewed and the successful continuation and expansion of the business. Decision making, then, among the managers surveyed was taking place within a framework of relatively consistent internal and external factors (production methods, operative performance, market needs, costs and pricing) well known to, but rarely articulated formally by, managers. Rather, all these factors were a natural part of the largely local and tactical arenas of managers.

Because the operational methods were longstanding, and thus eminently well known to staff, managers were engaged primarily on monitoring activities, scanning for deviations and taking a stream of small, though vital, decisions to keep the various functions operating satisfactorily. Large-scale or strategic propositions pertaining to a major change of method were not mentioned by managers. There was, then, a high level of 'certainty' among managers. Although bemoaning the lack of major decision making, at least they knew where they stood. This ingrained 'certainty' bolstered managerial authority in their local and tactical terrains, especially as there were few 'professionals' in terms of technology, production, distribution or management development who might challenge their realms.

At operational levels increased data speed, and accessibility, and to a less extent, better reliability of data, all related to increased IT, were quoted as improving decisions. Certainly these factors allowed faster response to internal and external influences (in the factory to absentee-ism and required changes in production schedules; in the warehouse to requirements of shops). This faster data speed came from data reformat-ting by the computer, in producing print-outs and the availability of instant data base interrogation. (No electronic mail as such was available in the company.) As has been noted elsewhere, increased data speed and increased data accessibility were themselves stimulating managers to request more of the same. There appeared to be some increase in uncertainty partly because of the early, but growing, awareness among managers of the potential for change that IT conferred.

Summary of IT effects

The whole process of designing fashion clothes on a seasonal basis, the consequent rapidity of detailed change of product, the virtually exclu-sively manual production and the relative looseness of systems and structures at Fashion are in striking contrast to the engineering com-panies previously described. These differences in culture and structure seem to parallel the differences in the products: flexible fabrics at Fashion, mechanical metals at the other two companies.

The take-up of IT and its effects on managers are obviously much influenced by Fashion's culture. There is no automation, robotics or electronic mail and only one personal computer. Systems are generally not sophisticated and computerization has been applied in only a limited way. The company is thus at an early stage in its IT trajectory. Virtually all practices are traditional and perhaps clung to by managers with a long and successful experience in the 'rag' trade. Throughout the discussions with managers rang the theme of the new computer systems conflicting with the established order.

Nevertheless, IT is directly changing the areas to which it has been applied. It is an increasing element in the roles of factory and warehouse management. Their operational routines are tightening, with more precise and clearer data informing their work. Information manage-ment, though these managers would not call it that, is slowly becoming more central. Data access, reliability, quantity, clarity, format and use-fulness are now matters of daily debate—undoubtedly stimulated by the spreading IT systems.

Not surprisingly, especially as there is little senior management con-sideration of IT planning, computer systems have as yet been merely superimpositions on existing paper-based arrangements. Also to be expected, the new computer systems, with extremely limited terminal access to user-managers produces masses of print-outs, an indigestible menu to managers more accustomed to discussion on the shop floor. Managers are accommodating the tightening operational procedures but with reluctance. They are also aware of the increasing visibility through IT that senior managers have of their operations. Thus junior and middle managers are giving less attention and time to 'social' management, which until latterly has been the core of their work. Their jobs, however, remain very much the same: busy, fragmented, oral and with high emphasis on keeping the work flowing. The senior managers are hardly affected directly by IT, but even they, on deeper reflection, usually confirmed their emphasis was now more on information management.

Case D—Integral

The company

Integral is a medium-sized company designing, manufacturing and marketing computing and communication systems. It is the result of a series of mergers and take-overs so convoluted that it is difficult to trace the lineage. Part of a giant federal corporation, Integral is expected to stand on its own feet, but success has been hard to come by. In 1985 yet another reorganization took place with lay-offs and management restructuring. Currently 1,200 people are employed on two sites.

The company designs integrated systems for a diversity of applications in industry, commerce, research and defence, and although computer hardware and software are the products, the emphasis is on designing appropriate systems. Components and sub-assemblies are bought-in, and 'manufacturing' consists of wiring and assembling items to form the finished computing and telecommunications equipment. Twenty managers were interviewed, and of these, fourteen returned questionnaires. In addition one non-interviewed manager completed the questionnaire (see Figure 4.7).

Tier 1	1	Managing director	1
Tier 2	5	General manager	1
Tier 3	3	Finance	1
Tier 4	7	Technical	5
Tier 5	4	Production	5
Total	20	Computing services	2
		Marketing	1
		Personnel	3
		Facilities	1
		Total	20

Figure 4.7 Pattern of surveyed managers

IT implementation

Integral is one of 200 companies comprising the corporation, which is headed by a chairman of considerable stature. During the 1960s and 1970s the corporation was created by many mergers and take-overs of companies diverse in size, products, markets, profitability and management style, but all in the broad field of electrics.

There is a clear corporate business policy—to maximize financial returns while allowing high autonomy to management of the individual companies in terms of products, markets and personnel. Financial indices are scrutinized by corporate central executives continually and explanations of figures sought of company managers at any time.

In Integral, and also in Components, the other electronics company, it was much more difficult to discover the pattern of implementation than in the other three cases. Naturally, electronics is fundamental to both companies, but IT for managerial processes does not necessarily have a strong visibility in contexts where IT is the product and is also used widely within the design and production processes. For instance, in Integral there is a long tradition of using computers in technical design of hardware and software, certainly since 1967. CAD (computer aided design) is essential there for printed circuit boards and other components.

Looking now at IT for managerial purposes: the corporation had set up a 'central' computer services company at a distant site which offered a menu of services at a price to other constituent companies. The forerunner of Integral began to purchase some of these services on a small scale around 1975, and this process has gradually extended, the initiative being apparently left to individual department managers.

The paradox (a word which springs easily to mind in considering IT) of Integral is that the company is centred upon electronics, with many IT experts and products, yet IT in the management arena had been guided by little planning or senior management interest. The functional managers had been left to take their own initiatives about computer systems, and not surprisingly the diffusion and use of these has been patchy and spasmodic. Nor has there been real attention to training of managers in this field or organization design catering for possible IT systems.

In implementation then, Integral is quite different from the non-electronic environments of the two mechanical engineering companies where management applications of IT are following a planned, if patchy, development. Here, in spite of the extent of IT expertise, and availability of hardware within the company, computer systems have been bought in, and 'bolted-on' with low commitment from managers.

The character of managers' work

Throughout the interviews it was clear that although the company was heavily involved in information technology, managers gave little importance to IT *as a management tool* or saw it as a major change force in the company. Overwhelmingly, achieving a future viable product range, the relative failure of a key current product, and above all, the current re-organization held their attention.

The managers interviewed were divided into three groups: systems experts (from a management viewpoint) (A), of which there were two; managers well implicated in IT activities (B/C); and managers little involved, or not involved, in IT-based work (D). (See Figures 4.8 and 4.9.) Managers were in general more involved in IT-based activities than in the three companies discussed previously, but as Integral is solely

a. | Tier | Questionnaires | | | Interviews | | |
|---|---|---|---|---|---|---|
| | A | B/C | D | A | B/C | D |
| 1 & 2 | – | 1 | 1 | – | 1 | 4 |
| 3 | – | 1 | 2 | 1 | 1 | 2 |
| 4 | – | 2 | 4 | 1 | 2 | 4 |
| 5 | – | 3 | – | – | 3 | 1 |
| Totals | – | 7 | 7 | 2 | 7 | 10 |

Questionnaires: 14　　　Interviews: 19
(1 from non-
interviewed manager;
13 from interviewed
managers)

Total group = 20 managers

b. | Function | Questionnaires | | | | | Interviews | | | | |
|---|---|---|---|---|---|---|---|---|---|---|
| | Tier | | | | | Tier | | | | |
| | 1/2 | 3 | 4 | 5 | Total | 1/2 | 3 | 4 | 5 | Total |
| MD and Gen. man. | 1 | | | | 1 | 2 | | | | 2 |
| Finance | | | 1 | | 1 | | | 1 | | 1 |
| Technical | | 1 | 1 | 1 | 3 | | 2 | 1 | 1 | 4 |
| Manufacturing | | 1 | 2 | 2 | 5 | | 1 | 3 | 2 | 6 |
| Marketing | | | | | | 1 | | | | 1 |
| Systems | 1 | | | | 1 | 1 | | 1 | | 2 |
| Personnel | 1 | 1 | 1 | | 3 | 1 | 1 | 1 | | 3 |
| Totals | 3 | 3 | 5 | 3 | 14 | 5 | 4 | 7 | 3 | 19 |

Figure 4.8　Pattern of interviews and questionnaires

engaged on IT design and IT product manufacturing, care had to be taken to distinguish between *technical* use of IT and its *managerial* use.

As in the other companies, the apparent involvement of managers varied widely, and was function related. Only in manufacturing was there a distinct expressed awareness of IT-induced change. What was especially noticeable in an electronics company was the sparse use of electronic mail, even though there were many references to geographic and functional isolation. This is in complete contrast to the situation at Components, where e-mail was used in a commonplace way.

As found in all the companies, managers appeared to have highly fragmented work, and it did appear that pace and fragmentation were associated. Time for reflection was not considered to have much changed. Neither was there hard evidence that the degree of proactivity had altered in ways related to IT. The overall impression was that each function had an historic character in terms of proactivity–reactivity and that character continued independent of the extent of IT usage.'

a.

Function	A	B/C	D	Total
MD & Gen. man.			2	2
Finance			1	1
Technical	1	3	1	5
Manufacturing		4	2	6
Marketing		1		1
Systems	1			1
Personnel			4	4
Totals	2	8	10	20

b.

	B/C	D
VDU in office: per manager	.8	.5
Personal computer: per manager*	0	0
Number of packages used daily	2.0	.3
Hours/week in systems issues	1.5	.9
Minutes/day on terminal or PC	100.3	7.5
Electronic messages sent/day	.4	.2

*(Note: some managers comment in the text about PCs obtained after this survey was taken.)

Figure 4.9 IT involvement[†] of managers

[†]Involvement primarily discriminated on time spent on systems issues, on direct use of terminals or personal computers, on electronic mail usage and on apparent amount of interaction with computer produced data.

The re-organization of the company, the redundancies and the lack of business success over recent years contributed to the uncertainty about the future direction of the company and probably heavily conditioned managers in their comments about the relatively formal planning components of their roles. Fifty per cent of managers claimed they now gave more emphasis to strategy, 60 per cent thought they were focusing on a longer time horizon and 85 per cent said the planning elements of their roles had increased. Undoubtedly computer systems in manufacturing were forcing a more disciplined planning approach. However, as was found elsewhere there was thought to be less planning of their own time, with IT prompting more reactivity.

Managers and people

With the one hundred people made redundant in January 1985, the total reduction in staff since 1980 was 33 per cent. Sixty per cent of interviewed managers said numbers of people at shop floor and in clerical positions had reduced. However, it proved impossible to link IT directly with these reductions because of the changed boundaries in functions and alterations in job titles. Undoubtedly the main reason for a smaller labour force was a reduced order book. Nevertheless there were areas where increasing IT was patently lowering the labour required for a given output.

The current pattern of manager responsibility is shown in Figure 4.10. By far the larger numbers of total staff reporting to a manager were in the manufacturing area. No hard evidence was forthcoming that the numbers of other managers reporting directly to a particular manager had changed, though most interviewees felt the total number of people within their responsibility had decreased.

Tier	No. of staff reporting directly to manager		No. of staff manager responsible for:
	Mean	Range	Range
1/2	4	2–7	8–540
3	4	1–6	2–161
4	4.5	2–5	2–160
5	3.5	3–4	11–43

Figure 4.10 Manager responsibilities for people

SKILLS OF PEOPLE

Managers commonly quoted downward trends in proportions of un-skilled and semi-skilled staff and upward trends in the proportion of skilled and professional staff. Often managers talked of difficulties in recruiting, and holding, the necessary highly qualified and experienced IT and systems staff, though there did not appear to be a personnel plan to cultivate management practices which might address this problem. (This was in contrast to the situation found at the other electronics company, Components, described in the next section.)

Because of the rapid technological advances, technical training had always received emphasis and was regarded as satisfactory by technical managers. However, training was regarded as weak throughout the company especially in the area of management and supervision and also in ongoing preparation for increasing management systems.

PEOPLE MANAGEMENT

Integral was essentially a 'high-tech' company: it had traditionally been technology-led, and other functions felt themselves to be subordinate and responsive to the technical needs of product and of customers. In virtually every interview this orientation was conspicuous. Questions in the 'people-management' area were largely answered blandly. No change was reported, for instance, in the 'management of people' content of their immediate subordinates and little change in their own time on 'people' issues, in time spent talking with their immediate subordinates or in the formality of their roles.

Managers and communication

As in all the studied companies communication was patently a key component in all managers' roles. Managers frequently reported that data issues were central and large in their work.

STRUCTURAL ISSUES

The two rather distinct markets, namely commercial and military, impart a bipartisan flavour to the operation, especially as the two group-ings are on separate sites, twenty-five miles apart. Further, head office is located at the 'Haydonwood' plant, and there was a definite feeling among managers at 'Southtown', where most of the interviews were conducted, that they were isolated from the main-stream of the company. There was little use of e-mail to reduce this isolation which was in contrast to the e-mail usage at Components, the other electronics company. In fact, there were many strong dissimilarities between these two companies even though their products, personnel and size were comparable. It was especially noticeable that the company culture regarding using IT for management purposes was entirely different and has engendered a rather limited and lack-lustre utilization in Integral, but a widespread and enthusiastic use in Components—seen for example in electronic communications. Also, at Integral, as the computer assistance was bought in from the corporation's 'Services' company, with decisions—in keeping with policy—being left to department heads, there appeared to be a low systemic cohesion between function-based systems, for instance between design and costing.

The whole picture was one of geographical and functional isolation, with departments able to be self-contained. Data crossed boundaries, because that was necessary, but there was a widespread tendency for managers to be less than positive about other departments. In particular it became clear that the company was driven from technical function, from which came the principal forces for success or failure of products.

There was little evidence of IT altering this pattern. Decisions on hiring-in packages from the 'Services' company seemed to have been taken without an overall cross-company policy. E-mail, although technically well understood and available, was used only slightly. Managers hardly mentioned it as an important management aid (again in contrast to Components). IT seemed not to have changed the apparent degree of integration or amount of boundary crossing. However, it was clear that the nature of the product (that is IT-based) *was* causing a deeper integration of quality (control) into both the design and manufacturing functions.

DATA ISSUES

Ninety-two per cent of surveyed managers felt their involvement with information gathering, analysis and dissemination had increased, and three-quarters perceived the quantity of data they were using had increased over recent years; this was especially noticeable among managers most involved with IT usage.

Questions regarding information flow (difficulties in knowing with whom to communicate; understanding by senior managers of work done; time spent dealing with other departments; amount of consultation with more senior managers) in relation to IT use all provoked 'no change' replies. However, the access of immediate subordinates to information available to their managers and time spent talking with immediate subordinates were both claimed to have increased. But neither of these issues could be ascribed to IT.

ORAL COMMUNICATION

Although it was impossible to derive quantitative data, managers in this company seemed to be less oral than in the other three companies so far described. This may be related to the high theoretical value embedded in the product and its design and manufacturing. There was a high amount of 'thinking' time on the part of technical managers and this coupled with the relative independence of departments, and the low numbers of manual and unskilled personnel, may have contributed to the impression of lower oral communication. (In 'Components' oral communication was extremely strong.)

Managers and decision making

Integral was a relatively small company of a large and complex corporation, whose board allowed high autonomy to local management, but closely and continuously monitored financial results. Little policy specific to integral appeared to emanate from the corporate board (apart from the need to maintain financial success measured by a cluster of known indicators), though directors of Integral implied that they had guidelines from above not necessarily known by their subordinate managers. Management within Integral was therefore responsible for developing and maintaining its own strategies, policies, management methods and styles.

The spheres of 'uncertainty' and 'decision making', as with all management activities, are fundamentally conditioned by the overall culture. While the financial expectations of the corporate board were an essential element in that culture, it is a reasonable assumption that the extant milieu at Integral, in which decision making was taking place, was principally the creation of the relatively few senior managers involved over recent years.

As discussed earlier, managers at Integral seemed uncertain about long-term plans. The lack of integration of Integral into the corporate cloth was reflected in a similar lack of integration within the company. Each function operated largely as a separate entity within its own sub-culture. The predominant sub-culture was 'technical', staffed by highly qualified and technologically specific people and orientated almost entirely toward the design and development of the product. Other functions were overshadowed by 'technical' and were attempting to be responsive to their needs. Little marketing or customer orientation was expressed anywhere.

There was, then, a high level of uncertainty among managers at the time of this study, partly short term, due to recent redundancies and a total re-organization, but probably mainly longer term. Certainly, virtually all the managers felt that they were not involved in long-term decisions and that there was no explicit strategy for IT. Often this latter thought was coupled in a bemused way with observations about the company having the technological expertise, but not applying it for management purposes.

A derivative of this apparent lack of longer-term considerations was the lack of emphasis on management systems and a lack of coherence between systems which were often mentioned. User-managers had not been involved in designing, or even contributing to the design, of systems.

At Integral, neither e-mail nor personal computers were widely used, so these potential tools for increasing data handling speed were relatively absent. (Both of these were seen as important components in relation to decision making in other companies.)

Summary of IT effects

Consequent upon market difficulties over several years, Integral was in the throes of a radical re-organization during this study; hence IT and its effects was not uppermost in managers' minds.

The company is long established in the IT business and thus managers are well versed in the hardware and software technologies. This is a situation distinctly different from the other companies previously described. In spite of this widespread understanding there was no apparent plan for IT use in management processes apart from a policy to buy-in externally designed packages. Using computers in technical design has, however, been standard for twenty years. A highly integrated system is being introduced into manufacturing management and it is in this function that most effects are noted.

Mangers rarely give importance to IT as a management tool although they perceive their IT involvement as increased with benefits to effectiveness. Where IT is used it provides more data, more rapidly, but there are problems of relevance. There is little evidence that IT may change the sub-culture of any function—pace, the degree of reactivity, fragmentation all seemed strongly related to the function itself. No evidence emerges that IT is changing the degree of integration between functions or time horizons.

Numbers of unskilled and semi-skilled people are felt to be decreasing as a consequence of IT, though exact numbers were not forthcoming, partly because of other concurrent changes, while the proportion of skilled and professional staff seems to be increasing. Technical training is regarded as satisfactory but little priority is given to management development or preparation for IT.

There is a distinct feeling of isolation, at 'Southtown', associated with distance from Head Office and with product division, and although the technology is available, it is not being used to address this problem. Most managers feel their involvement with information processes has increased over recent years and this is most noticeable among IT-involved managers, who feel data timeliness has improved. Within manufacturing greater integration and organizational transparency is noted.

Integral has a somewhat indefinite milieu regarding decisions, possibly associated with lack of financial success recently. The lack of coherent systems is also often mentioned. Speed of data handling is seen positively in decision making. Most managers feel decisions have become more complex, but their decision-making authority is unchanged.

IT is being applied in few management areas, and only in those areas are there identifiable implications for management roles. The non-IT forces in this case (lack of business success, the consequent re-organization and historical culture) far outweigh any implications of information technology.

Integral is very different from the other companies already described in that managers have a high level of technological understanding of electronics and software. In spite of this, the emphasis placed on this arena by managers is no higher than within Engineering and Hardwear. Changes produced by IT implementation in Integral seem to be fewer than in those companies, though patterns of change are similar. Once again, immediate effects appear to be dependent on local contexts. The later and deeper consequences for organizational culture, structure and processes emerge as basically similar to the other cases.

Case E—Components

The company

Components is a British site at 'Ouseford' employing 2,300 people of an American-based multi-national whose business is designing, manufacturing and marketing electronic components, assemblies of these and systems. IT has been used for decades and is an inherent and major factor in the organization.

The company's products are marketed to other electronics companies or direct to user-customers. Rate of change of technology, both of product and of manufacturing, is rapid, and market demand fluctuates greatly year-on-year. The technical change rate requires high responsiveness and personnel and organizational flexibility—characteristics which pervade the company. Organization charts were not available; reporting and responsibility patterns appeared to be a 'dynamic matrix', adjusting to internal and external requirements.

	Interviews	Questionnaires (non-interviewed Managers)	Totals
Tier 1	–	–	–
Tier 2	3	7	10
Tier 3	12	13	25
Tier 4	2	1	3
Total	17	21	38

	Interviews	Questionnaires (not interviewed)	Totals
General managers	1	4	5
Finance	1	3	4
Technical	2	2	4
Manufacturing	3	3	6
Marketing	5	6	11
Systems	1	1	2
Personnel*	4	2	6
Total	17	21	38

*Includes: 1—legal, 1—buildings maintenance

Figure 4.11   Pattern of surveyed managers

At the site are located finance, research, technical customer support, manufacturing, marketing, data processing, personnel and other services functions. Seventeen managers were interviewed and of these seven also returned questionnaires. In addition twenty-one non-interviewed managers returned questionnaires (giving a total of twenty-eight questionnaires). Tier positions appeared difficult for managers themselves to define, job titles seemed not to be specific and were little guide (to an outsider) of the job content (see Figure 4.11).

IT implementation

There appears to be a strong belief in this plant that the company 'knows where it is going'. This confidence among interviewed managers in company policies and long-term thinking is in marked contrast to the situation perceived at the other four companies. At Components managers spontaneously referred to an extant strategic plan—for products, markets, personnel and for information technology.

The entire environment at Components was technological and electronic. With nearly sixty years of continuous research, development and application of sophisticated electronics and nearly forty years of computer hardware and software involvement, the company's staff regarded IT as commonplace. Paradoxically, they also usually expressed feelings of wonder about the potential and the 'magic' of the technology. All interviewed managers appeared to have a good inherent knowledge of computers and telecommunications—the heart of the business—though naturally depth of understanding varied depending on the manager's background. However, the level of awareness of the possibilities of the technology must be regarded as of a high order (and much higher than in the other four companies). Of the seventeen interviewed managers fifteen had degrees, HNDs or HNCs; of the eleven who had degrees, eight were in electronics or physics and two in technology.

Two characteristics of the business surfaced often: the pace of technological developments and the volatility of the market place. Thus, while there were strategic plans internationally, for product and manufacturing process development, and for marketing, the company was always flexing to cope with market or technical changes. Thus *flexibility* and *responsiveness* were organizational attributes absolutely needed to maintain viability.

Because of this ambience of technicality, rapid developments, flexibility and responsiveness, it was difficult to separate electronic activities related to product and process design and development and those related to management. In fact, demarcations of any kind were not easy to discern. Powerful computer analysis, widespread networking, easily available printouts, instantaneous world-wide communication, personal computers and terminals were available to all the managers and were used in all functions.

There had been certain strategies for IT for many years—for instance, world-wide standards for hardware and for international linkages. Similarity in certain technological activities and some management areas (for instance, finance) software and formatting protocols had been standardized for years.

In spite of this high level of strategic thinking there did not appear to be a coherent plan for using IT as a management tool at 'Ouseford'. The potential for this application was well understood, but managers generally tended to be overwhelmed by the availability of technical resources and seemed not to focus on the management applications and implications. In a sense, as will be discussed later, the overall frenetic pace at Components while conferring advantages in some ways, appeared to militate against long-term thinking and coherence of management development.

Discrimination in the use of IT (as a management tool) between functions proved to be impossible. All functions seemed to have a similar level of general IT usage, and as mentioned earlier, distinctions between functions, on any matter, were difficult to ascertain.

The character of managers' work

The average age of the interviewed group was thirty-seven (and of the managers returning questionnaires, thirty-nine), with an average time in the company of eleven years and incumbency in present position of three years. Managers had moved around the company widely. C-6 was quite typical: degree in physics; thirty-nine years of age; four years with another electronics company; then twelve years with Components; quality assurance engineer; then product engineering; then research and development team manager; then general manager of a product group.

IT INVOLVEMENT WITH MANAGERS

As has been described, managers at Components used information technology in a commonplace way. It proved difficult to differentiate managers by their degree of involvement in IT first because of the predominance of electronics backgrounds (see Figure 4.13) among staff, and second because of the abundance of IT facilities. The extent to which a particular manager was knowledgeable about the technical aspects of IT or usage of hardware or of software was no guide to involvement in IT-based management systems or awareness of them. (This was a feature also of the other electronics company Integral, and distinctively different from the situation in the other three non-electronic companies where knowledge of IT usually, though not always, meant knowledge of its use in a management context.)

Using the same discriminators as for the other four companies—time spent on systems issues, direct use of terminals or personal computers, electronic mail usage, and apparent amount of interaction with computer-produced data—an attempt was made to separate managers into two major groups. B/C managers appeared to have a higher IT involvement than D managers as shown in Figure 4.12. However, as discussed later, the *behaviour* of B/C managers and D managers as revealed by the questionnaire survey appeared to be similar on most

	B/C	D
VDU in office: per manager	.6	.3
PC in office: per manager	.4	.1
Number of packages used daily	1.9	.2
Hours per week on system issues	1.6	.8
Minutes per day on terminal or PC	6	3.4
Electronic messages sent/day	8	10

Figure 4.12 IT involvement of managers

Interviewed group				Questionnaire group (not interviewed)			
HNCs HNDs	Degrees	Higher degrees	Physics; electronics; technology	HNCs HNDs	Degrees	Higher degrees	Physics; electronics; technology
4	11	3	10	6	15	3	9
	Out of total of 17				Out of total of 21		

Figure 4.13 Qualifications of managers

issues, and indeed there was much more commonality than among similar groups in the other four companies.

In spite of the electronics environment in which the managers had operated for years, personal computers, electronic mail and systems issues appeared in 40 per cent of comments regarding major sources of change in the company over the past five years. Personal computers were one of two vectors (the other being organizational restructuring) most frequently quoted as producing substantial change. The speed of change of the technology and the variability of the market were also often quoted sources of change.

Virtually all managers claimed their involvement with, and knowledge of, systems and computers had risen substantially over the recent past, as had their usage of electronic data bases. Information gathering, analysis and dissemination was also widely perceived as having increased. IT, then, had become a fundamental and perhaps an essential component of the management method.

PACE

Fifty per cent of returned questionnaires claimed that job pace was 20 per cent higher than five years previously, and 61 per cent thought time for reflection was down 10–20 per cent, though there was no difference for these issues between managers highly involved in IT and those who were less so. By observation, there was no doubt that the pace at Components was high and much higher than in the other four companies. Managers usually made clear that they wanted every second to count in the interviews: they were open, cooperative, but wasted little time on 'off the ball' subjects. The pressure and pace in the company was apparent at all times and in all situations—in telephone calls, in arrangements for meetings, and in managers' descriptions of their activities. It seemed that throughout the company there was pressure to work quickly, to get things done, to avoid time-wasting. Hectic pace was endemic, with little time for reflection, and the increasing application of

IT was perceived as speeding up activities even more. Several factors seemed to be associated with this apparent acceleration: virtual instantaneous interconnection of managers and technologists throughout the site and throughout the world, improvement in timeliness of data (ie arriving in time to be useful)—quoted by more than half the surveyed managers—and the much greater use of computer data bases perceived by 75 per cent of managers.

The production system had become increasingly complex in terms of the different sub-processes which could be combined several ways to produce the range of products. These complexities had reached a point years ago when product design, quality control, batch tracking (etc.), could *only* be handled by computer. The discretion to choose to use a computer had disappeared—it had to be used. Similarly, in other functional areas, PM systems were unable to cope with the complexity and the cost penalties of slow response. Again, computers and telecommunications were the sole option. IT applications, once installed, diminished slack time and slack resources: perceived (and probably actual) organizational pace increased.

ROLE SPECIFICATION

No manager offered a printed organization chart, and while there appeared to be clarity in terms of business objectives, definition of roles tended to be loose. Proactivity was obviously a dominant element in the culture: managers were expected to take initiatives. This freedom of action must, however, be set in the context of highly systematic reporting procedures and company policies, both of which appeared to be known well and generally accepted and practised. (46 per cent of surveyed managers claimed the number of rules and regulations in their job had increased.) Work fragmentation was high: managers frequently mentioned pace, changes of direction, responsiveness and flexibility. In addition there was encouragement for managers to consult freely within the site, and outside the site, on all kinds of issues.

All these factors contributed to virtually no role specifications: rather each role was self-defined and changing often and rapidly to deal with the contingent situation. Managers claimed their amount of 'routines' had not altered over recent years. Also, there was no difference perceived in routines changing between the 'IT-involved' and the 'less-involved' groups. Generally managers had great problems with recall of how they used their time. This was common in all five companies but was more pronounced in Components, and while in most cases there were recurring activities, for instance weekly meetings, the overwhelming impression was of reaction to events but in a proactive way. In other words, once the stimulus of a problem or opportunity had occurred, the manager had high proactive freedom to deal with it.

Clearly, managers in Components were using electronic mail to a much greater extent than five years before, and this conferred greater transparency to the organization. Throughout every day streams of messages were being received by each manager—prompting action and usually the dispatch of more messages. (This will be dealt with later under communications.) The message stream informed and interrogated the manager, thus stimulating and restimulating action. Although the culture endorsed proactivity, the apparent effect of electronic messaging was to produce higher reactivity, the 'urgency' of priorities tending to take preference over 'importance'. The impression was that electronic mail, while valued by managers, was probably tending to increase fragmentation, and pace, and to decrease role specificity.

PLANNING

Two-thirds of managers felt the planning elements in their roles had increased and that they gave more emphasis to strategy, as distinct from short-term tactics. The time ahead on which managers focused was also said to be greater than it was five years before. Managers were required to make estimates of business indices at prescribed future periods and this data was integrated to form product group, country and world-wide plans. Here, the computer system was tightening disciplines of timing, format and requirements for action on managers, in terms of the formal planning protocols.

However, within their informal (and as previously described, pacey, fragmented and unroutine) roles, most managers appeared to give a low priority to planning and to regret that. It would seem from this that IT was having two opposed effects. Formal planning was disciplined by virtue of the computer-driven system, but individual managers appeared to be more focused by IT on the immediate, with a consequent weakening of personal informal planning.

BOUNDARIES

Boundaries, both vertical and functional at Components, appeared to be easily crossed. The company practised a 'single status' policy in conditions of employment and this was expressed in common arrangements for office layouts, car parking and refectory. No organization charts were in evidence and job titles generally contained no indicator of status; indeed to an outsider it was difficult to classify managers either by status or function from job titles. There appeared to be a tacit understanding that all functions contributed to the well-being and success of the company. Further, integration between functions seemed to be necessary for success. Thus managers communicated freely with

anyone they believed to be useful to the situation. The culture traditionally encouraged boundary crossing. (This is discussed under Communication, later.) The widespread use of electronic mail, and of cross-
functional data bases, augmented boundary crossing and the insubstan-
tiality of boundaries.

Managers and people

NUMBERS OF PEOPLE

It proved impossible to link changes in numbers of staff specifically to
use of IT. Obtaining historical data on numbers employed, on turnover
and profit and loss, was not possible. Further, market fluctuations and
the rapidity of product and process change meant that internal restructuring was a continuing process. Thus numbers of people in particular
sections were associated much more with designed alterations of business practice (for instance reporting patterns or methods of production)
than to applications of IT. Spans of responsibility are shown in Figure
4.14. Both Tier 2 and Tier 3 managers reported that numbers of people

	Numbers of staff reporting directly to manager			Numbers of staff manager responsible for		
Tier	Mean	Most common range*	Range	Mean	Most common range*	Range
2	5.6	4–6	4–10	172	30–150	5–650
3	5.5	3–7	1–23	40	14–53	1–188
4	3.0	–	–	3	–	–

*80 per cent of managers in this range

Figure 4.14 Manager responsibilities for people

reporting to their first-line supervisors had risen over the previous five
years.

The assumption running through most interviews was that IT had
vast potential for increasing the success of the company—particularly in
fast analysis and fast communication—and should be used wherever
possible. This 'added-value' theme suggested the company was on a
later stage of the implementation curve in which staff *effectiveness* was
the predominant issue rather than staff reduction.

SKILLS OF PEOPLE

Components is a highly technological company: its managers are well qualified, usually science or technologically experienced and there are many technical staff. Three-quarters of the surveyed group of managers felt that the number of professionals and skilled people among their subordinates had increased over the preceding five years. The impression frequently given was of an increasingly complex business, technically, economically and organizationally. The key orientation which continually emerged was data—acquisition, analysis and dissemination. Not surprisingly then, discussion of skills of subordinates was often focused on this same theme. Although, naturally, skills in functional areas, that is in personnel, finance, marketing and production (etc.) were also prime. C-6 (a general manager) was obviously concerned about the development of his subordinates and the balance between business needs and people needs. He was bothered that he himself was not well skilled in PC use and data management and trying to decide whether he should be more skilled. Here was a case where subordinates were more skilled at accessing and analysing business data than their manager.

For most managers interviewed it was clear that conceptual and system skills, in relation to data (knowing what programs were available, how to access programs and related data and being skilled in understanding revealed information), were of high importance. This pattern of work was apparent in several other sections and was characterized by managerial and non-managerial roles being similar and subordinates having high access to data via terminals. Indeed, 75 per cent of managers in the study thought the access of their immediate subordinates to information available to themselves had increased over recent years. (There was no difference between 'IT-involved', and 'less-involved' managers on this point.)

TRAINING

Clearly the pace of technological change forced an inherent learning posture on most professional and technical staff. Almost always when training was mentioned by managers, it implied a technical context. The impression given was that management training and development was not a priority. Indeed, the whole canvas of data science and management seemed not to have received deep attention. To specific questions, managers often said they themselves had had little exposure to management courses.

There appeared to be a vigorous 'training-by-doing' environment for all levels of staff. Job competence was obviously linked with other factors such as salary and promotion. Reviews of staff were systematic, and those within the bottom quartile of the range were counselled to improve or sometimes to alter their career routes. Again, these underlying structures, putting emphasis on performance, appeared to be motivating staff to work hard for long hours and to encourage self-help in discovering how to get things done.

MANAGEMENT OF PEOPLE

While each of the companies studied had a unique culture, that at Components seemed to be much 'stronger' and ubiquitous: staff at all levels expressed similar views of 'how things are done around here'. Verbal expressions of company styles and policy and the behaviour of managers (in interviews and from observation) and of secretaries, technicians, switchboard operators and receptionists together created an image of a coherent and self-assertive culture. Many influences obviously had contributed and were still contributing to the nature of this culture, one of them being the fast-moving technology of its products. It has to be emphasized that even though the products of Integral and Components were similar, their cultures were totally dissimilar.

Part of this sturdy culture at Components appeared to be a well thought out policy of people management. Naturally, the high-technology ambience required staff well educated in the relevant technologies, but quality in educational requirement and emphasis on careful selection was evident throughout the company. Young graduates were expected to engage in real issues almost from their day of appointment—all presented short briefings to the MD and personnel director on their current work within weeks of starting with the company. Youth was apparent throughout the organization: the MD and personnel director were under forty and the mean age of interviewed managers was thirty-seven.

The key emphasis was on hard work and commitment, and this translated into the fast pace, previously discussed, and the continual drive to achieve maximum output for minimum input. A disciplined staff appraisal system was used in which managers ranked all their staff. Feedback to staff also appeared to be well developed; thus there was a widespread understanding of what had to be done to earn high salaries and to gain promotion. The company practised a single-status policy, with low visibility or hierarchy, similar office space and furniture for all staff; 'first names' and informality abounded. The summation of all these factors created an organization completely different from the other four companies studied. While much of this ambience was 'designed-in' by adhering to policies presumably originating in the United States (and probably derived from the historical themes of the parent company), the interviewed managers ostensibly had internalized these ideas and their management style was a derivative thereof.

How is the increasing IT usage altering the management of people? Although some reduction of staff related to IT was quoted, and while head-count and productivity were obviously vital, most managers had the same numbers of staff as five years previously, while the proportion of professional and skilled staff had generally risen.

Technically well-qualified managers were thus managing technically well-qualified, or technically skilled, personnel. The greater spread of terminals, PCs and access to data meant these skilled subordinates had opportunities to use equipment, to interrogate data bases and to use electronic mail in the same manner as their managers—and indeed in some cases more than their managers. Thus, the impression was that the differences between managers and non-managers (already designed-in to be low in visibility) were reducing, due to IT, in ways which were central to management, that is in relation to information access and control.

Managers and communication

With the abundance of facilities both for electronic processing of data, and for its transmission by e-mail and the cultural disposition toward rich interactions between 'relevant people', communication might well be considered the quintessential feature of management at Components.

It is important to emphasize again the differences of communication content (hardness—softness), and of method (systematic IT-based and oral) discussed in chapter two. Components is highly sophisticated in computer systems of all kinds and in all functions—and much more so than the other four companies studied. The impression was given that computer-based systems had been used and continuously modified over decades, with high commitment to these developments throughout management. Paper-based 'transaction processing' had largely disappeared many years previously: IT has become an integrated component of the total organizational process. Given the senior-level commitment to IT and the cultural norms of pace, responsiveness, proactivity, informality, hard work and achievement, and the electronic facilities, there was a universal zeal for communication and information management.

STRUCTURAL ISSUES

The culture of the organization encouraged informal contact with relevant persons irrespective of either functional boundaries or hierarchy. Organizational structure appeared to be dynamic and responsive to need. Again, the flexibility of IT systems, given the rich distribution of access via terminals, appeared to reinforce this flexibility. In fact IT increased the *range* of data sources and personal consultation for managers and thus the flexibility and responsiveness of the total system. Managers found delination of their communication patterns difficult— more so than in the other companies—the reactivity to e-mail, the pace and the 'open access' culture all undoubtedly contributed to this uncertainty.

Thus the extensive electronics system further increased the ease of data flow and data access, and this in turn organizational transparency—a feature commented upon by several managers. There was a degree of threat in this level of openness: senior managers were informed of issues as early as were section managers. Not only were specific functional indices exposed (for instance accounting measures) to senior levels, but this information stimulated interrogation of both the computer data base and other managers. E-mail allowed this rapid interrogation and created the expectation of fast response. An example of this mentioned by several managers was the world-wide accounting system using international index standards, enabling a range of monthly accounting measures for all plants to be available at head office (in the United States) and simultaneously to each relevant manager in each plant. This simultaneous availability of data, plus virtually instantaneous e-mail, allowed management analysis and understanding of the data to be considerably enhanced.

Another similar example was the systematic planning and budgeting procedures which required each manager to state financial, product and people targets for three months, one year and three years ahead. Once on the electronic data base, senior managers can explore these projec-tions in detail, and once again, using e-mail, can 'discuss' issues with section managers. Some managers had PCs at home so they could communicate with the corporation world-wide and managers frequently spoke of being in touch with the system (and the system with them) wherever they were—for instance on overseas visits. But there were dysfunctional effects of this ease of communication, as many managers implied. CQ-14 (technical):

Ease of exchange of technical information ensures better synergy among our world-wide technical teams (for example less duplication of effort). However, the result of this is that technical managers then need to spend more time digesting and analysing the vast quantities of data which they now can access.

IT then, was probably not altering the formal structures at Com-ponents, but was enhancing the extant dynamism of communications, communication patterns and changing the focus of attention of managers.

DATA ISSUES

In interviews managers talked of information and communication issues more than of any other subject. From the questionnaires, three-quarters of managers thought their involvement in information gathering, analysis and dissemination had increased in recent years, and 67 per cent felt their time chasing information had increased. This is another example of the 'positive feedback' of IT systems—although access is reputed to be faster and more widespread that itself appears to generate more information access problems. This is associated with *amounts* of information available, seen to have increased by 95 per cent of managers (70 per cent said paperwork had increased).

Data issues which surfaced commonly were information quantity and relevance. As discussed in chapter two, all data contain information: it is the art of analysis, reformatting and display which reveals it. With increasingly adroit electronic systems managers can restructure data to reveal arrays of relationships—for instance of product clusters, prices, costs and sales by geographic regions. But once again, what constituted optimum advantage? This question came up repeatedly. 'Shall we ever get the data we want? . . . Lots of data are on the main frame but are bureaucratically difficult to access . . . We probably see too much data— we have to learn to trim data dependent on what is currently important' (C-6). (Managers often used 'data' and 'information' interchangeably.)

This theme of too much data and the problem of deciding the relevance and utility of information ran through many interviews and was often coupled with two observations: first that the manager himself was not informed enough on systems design and second, that systems design had not sufficiently taken into account the users' needs.

Timeliness was claimed to have improved by many managers, though timeliness, data and quantity, relevance and ease of access are interactive in a complex way and not separated clearly in the perceptions of managers. 'Data timeliness is not improving due to *more* material being accessible' (C-1, marketing).

Another effect of IT is the creation of tight system-time disciplines (found in the other companies also), that is inputs to the system are required at specific dates. This time discipline imposes itself on the organization generally and anonymously and managers felt, and expressed, their need to stay within this time synchronization. The overwhelming implication of managers' statements was that the value of information had increased due to IT. Speed of transmission, ease of access, reliability and analytical and reformatting speed and power were quoted continuously. Often the impression was given that the directions and pace of developments could only have been maintained because of the spread and power of the electronics technology. That there were dysfunctional implications has been catalogued above—in increased paperwork, in sometimes frenetic responsiveness, in focus on immediate concerns, but the net effect expressed by all managers was positive.

ORAL COMMUNICATION

As in the other four companies, managers at Components were involved in much oral transactions—in the whole range of person-to-person communication—counselling, briefing, meetings and conversation. Indeed, the informal and 'team-like' relationships with both subordinates and superordinates were more characteristic of a research institution than a commercial company. Seventy per cent of managers felt their time talking with immediate subordinates and with more senior managers had increased in recent years, and while this may have been optimistic thinking, certainly there was no evidence that as IT systems extended oral communication contracted.

The summation of managers' comments portrayed a highly oral environment, informal, team-like, seemingly based on an underlying conviction that informing and being informed was a continuing necessity for success, personal and organizational.

Managers and decision making

DECISION ISSUES

As in all the companies, managers at Components found the arena of decision making the most difficult to recall and to delineate. There was little spontaneous reference to the subject, in contradistinction to the extemporaneous flows of comment on communication. There was, however, a high consensus (86 per cent) among the surveyed group that taking decisions had increased in complexity, though managers commonly gave the impression that everything had become more complicated. This was partly related to the multiple-reporting patterns, particularly the 'nestling boxes' structure (United Kingdom, Europe, world) and partly the 'communicate with everyone' mode.

As discussed earlier, the corporation had a well-understood strategic plan, and disciplined forward budgeting constructed by every manager and then integrated into a whole. It was clear that these two processes, top-down strategy and bottom-up budgeting (and planning), created a stabilizing framework containing the widespread and favoured initiative taking. Also there appeared to be definite guidelines for decision authority (61 per cent of managers thought their authority to take decisions had risen).

Everywhere pace was manifest. The combination of volatile market, speed of technological development and the fast electronic transaction capability combined to force rapid decisions. In fact, the culture acclaimed rapid decision making: responsiveness was regarded as a prime favourable attribute. As in other areas, it appeared that the use and availability of IT had paradoxical and sometimes opposite effects. The ability to consult widely and often, and to access powerful data bases rapidly, allowed a higher level of 'organizational intelligence' to be applied to situations. Examples were quoted of solutions to problems being available by fast access to 'expert' advice thousands of miles away, and it was obvious from observation that this process was continuous and widely used. On the other hand, the mass of information 'on tap' to managers was frequently mentioned as confusing or overwhelming and complicating the decision process. Further, incoming streams of messages via e-mail focused managers onto immediate issues—probably to the detriment of taking longer-term views. (In spite of this, managers felt their planning had increased and their time horizon had extended.)

The personal computer was widely identified as a new systems facilitator, allowing ease of access and use of programs and data, in contrast to the bureacracy and relative slowness of response of the mainframe system. Culturally favoured features of speed and responsiveness were enhanced by the PCs. One senior manager thought decision making

was quite sloppy—not far from careless. The technology may be driving us to worse decision making—there is not much introspection—not much probing, but a lot of speed. Actually the decision tight rope is not as narrow as we make out. We make fun of staid industries, but the high-technology industry is not universally manned by brilliant managers, . . . high tech specialists are often thoughtless and in too much of a hurry.

This man's comments well summarized the decision-making culture at Components. IT certainly conferred advantages, but as with many activities, the crucial feature was balance. The technical merits of speed, analysis and synthesis had to be balanced by managerial competencies and time to pursue and use them.

Summary of IT effects

In every way, Components is conspicuously different from the other companies. Its business has always been based on electronics technology and systems and its culture is innovatory. The use of IT is highly developed and is commonplace in all functions, though managers still regard it as a key source of change. Throughout, managers are deeply involved in IT-based information management and IT-based communication, and much more so than in the other four companies. Management and IT have become inextricably interwoven. The basic character of the work of managers, already treated several times in this book, is found in this company also. Inescapably, whatever the culture, jobs of managers are highly fragmented, unroutine and oral. If anything IT is reinforcing these fundamentals at Components.

As has been found elsewhere, the technology may produce opposing implications. For instance the ubiquity of access, and continual prompting of managers via terminals, pushes them towards reaction to short-term, tactical issues. On the other hand, the computer-managed mid-term planning and budgeting regime extends time focus. Interestingly, managers have a high acceptance of this tight and rather anonymous planning mechanism. Also the node-to-relevant-node communication engendered by IT stimulates initiative taking and weakens designatory structures. Thus IT, in this company, is enhancing both management reactivity and proactivity. Reaction is prompted by IT but once stimulated managers have wide scope for initiatives using IT.

The 'productivity vector' of IT is well understood among managers who are constantly pressing for improved performance. The number of staff for a given output is reducing, though in this company the 'added-value' orientation regarding the technology is highly developed. Skills of people are commonly believed to be increasing and changing, with managers and non-managers jobs becoming less different.

The abundance of IT facilities allows rapid communication throughout the site and throughout the world. Thus not only is transparency increased within the local management group (as in the other companies), in Components that transparency extends throughout the corporation. As found elsewhere, increase in transparency tends to cause feelings of vulnerability among managers.

In spite of the richness of technical communication, oral transactions continue unabated. In fact, as 'team' relationships are the norm at Components, and as status and functional inhibitions are not significant (partly because of IT), oral communication is even more manifest than in the other companies. Decision making was increasingly aided by part of the IT-driven information system. While information being easily and quickly available confers advantages to the decision processes, the IT-induced data overload produces problems of relevance, and at times, confusion for managers.

Each of the companies is, then, on its own 'IT trajectory', partially determined by the inherent qualities of the technology, but also determined in a major way by the particular organizational cultures. Fashion is patently in the very early stages of IT use; Components, on the other hand, has had a long experience of sophisticated computer-driven information systems and telecommunications. The other three companies fall between. But it would be over-simplistic to see the five companies lying on a smooth continuum representing their degree of IT sophistication. Rather, as a consequence of a multitude of pressures, internal and external, each had arrived at its own unique IT scenario at the time of this study. Each faces its own set of problems and opportunities, though, as the analysis in the next chapter will show, there are commonalities. There is much to be learnt from each case, not least that with extremely high levels of IT as at Components, there are disfunctional effects as the information overload on managers increases their problems of data priority and relevance.

5 Analysis

Managers reporting to me are more numerate—'people-orientated' managers may be decreasing and 'data-oriented managers may be increasing. [Director—Fashion]

IT is affecting my job greatly—the biggest problem is understanding the info the computer gives me—it's too much . . . we do not yet understand the system. [Production manager—Integral]

Introduction

The objective of this research is to improve understanding of the implications for managers of increasing diffusion and use of information technology in their companies. The analysis which follows is thematic, drawing ideas and material from across the five companies and integrating research findings with the key literature. There are three sections. First an introduction; then the implementation of IT in the companies is examined, especially in relation to managers; in the third section the implications for managers are characterized.

In spite of the five companies having many similarities, their uniqueness is striking. In every respect—in attitudes, structures and practices—each company has its own very different story. And, importantly for this research, each company has its own history of IT in terms of pace of introduction, choice of equipment, applications and impact on people and processes. Each company is, it seems, on its own IT 'trajectory'.

Fashion is the least developed in IT terms and in shop-floor mechanization. It is regarded as being in the very early stages of IT development with only slight effects on management work. Even though Integral is in electronics, and part of a giant multi-national, the use of IT for management purposes is not well developed; there, IT impact on managers is slight-to-medium. Engineering and Hardwear, both parts of multi-nationals, and with a long history of computing practices, have the greatest similarities. In both, IT is gathering momentum as a major change force and effects on managers are distinct and widespread.

Components is a different company from the others in all respects. It has long experience of sophisticated computer-driven information management and a culture which gives great weight to adaptation and initiative-taking. This organization is by far the most affected by IT and may give the best indication of future directions of IT implications for other companies.

Historically, technology has been predominantly associated with physical products and their production (see Macdonald *et al.*, 1983). Office activities and, specifically, management arenas have in contrast been largely non-technological in concept and in practice. Although precursors to IT have been infiltrating office settings for decades, it is only recently that management contexts and activities have been influenced substantially.

While the chosen companies are all in the manufacturing sector, the managers in this study are almost always in office settings, and in non-manufacturing functions such as accounting, marketing or personnel. Some production and factory managers are included, and naturally their work is closely associated with the shop floor. However, this research is primarily about managers in office settings. Although each company is different, the analysis shows that a coherent thesis about the diffusion of IT and its effects on managers is possible. It is presented in the rest of this chapter.

Implementation of information technology

Each company had its own unique history of precursors to IT. All had several decades of experience of telephones, telex, punched-card data processing and shop-floor mechanization. And except at Fashion, computing practices stretched back twenty to thirty years. Forms of 'work-study' and 'organization and methods' (O and M) had also been used in each company. There was then, no *tabula rasa*.

Company uniqueness naturally extended to all aspects of culture, structure and processes. In spite of the five organizations having common features—they are all in manufacturing, medium-to-large, situated in the same geographical area and have similar functional activities—their differences are the more striking. Such dissimilarities had been expected between Fashion, the garments company, and the four engineering businesses, and these were certainly revealed. But there are major contrasts among all the companies, especially (and significantly) between the two electronic companies.

It was also plain that the range of knowledge and experience of IT and enthusiasm for its application was wide among managers and professionals. As shown in chapter two IT has many forms in terms of hardware, software and usage, and a user-manager usually knew only those applications specific to his work context. The sample of managers interviewed was based on their involvement, albeit slight in some cases, in IT, and yet even these people were seldom knowledgeable about systems and computers. The lack of awareness of the advantages of using IT on the part of British managers reported (for instance) by Northcott and Rogers (1982) still seems to apply. Senior managers in the management information systems (MIS) function, although expert and enthusiastic about IT-driven systems, rarely had a complete company overview. Certainly, the common nature of electronic digital technology underlies and integrates diverse systems such as automation, robotics, computing and telecommunication. But the plurality of IT is also dominant. While the inherent characteristics of IT discussed in chapter two are important in determining its diffusion and use, the specific choices of equipment, software and mode of implementation are also vital.

Contention, but evolution

Godet (1986) argues that the current transition crisis in societies results from the opposition between technological and economic driving forces for change and inertial forces of social behaviour and structure for maintaining the status quo. This usefully describes what was found in this research. However, it would be simplistic to portray these tensions as linear. Rather, in each company there exists a multi-directional web of interests which is itself dynamic. As new technologically based activities are introduced, the accumulating experience changes the knowledge base and the enthusiasms of individuals. Technological and economic parameters of IT—vital ingredients in the unfolding—are also changing swiftly. These are altering the gross technical and economic disposition of IT-based systems compared with existing pre-IT arrangements. But they are, at the same time, changing the relative attractiveness of particular IT hardware and/or software as compared with others.

In each segment of the companies, therefore, the state of IT implementation is evolving as the result of contention between several technical, economic and contextual factors which may be grouped as:

1. the inherent technical characteristics of IT (discussed in chapter two), such as speed of operation, which result in actual or perceived economic advantages;
2. the relative technical and economic choices between competing IT alternatives.

(Both these are primarily promoted by, and argued about among IT experts.)

3. the unique company functional and hierarchical contexts represented by the wide range of managers, supervisors, professionals and staff; and various levels of sophistication of existing systems.

There are no discontinuities: rather the evidence everywhere is of gradualism as successive changes are made. However, it is clear that since about 1980 there has been an acceleration both in the spread of technology—hardware and software—and in the realization among managers of its potential for competitive advantages.

As suggested earlier two schools of thought on IT implementation are articulated in the literature. The 'rationalists' deriving from the Taylor tradition, see IT as a continuing and inevitable substitution of machines for people. Indeed, among this group, the pessimists believe the process will unerringly result in a decrease in jobs, degradation of work and an increase in social controls (Braverman, 1978; Barron and Curnow, 1979; Jenkins and Sherman, 1979). The second school takes a contingency approach, seeing the effects of IT as dependent on context (Land, in Piercy, ed., 1984; Bessant and Grunt, 1985).

What the research here indicates is that there is a certain determinism inherent in the characteristics of the technologies which is driving organizations and their managements in identifiable directions. But in the shorter run the patterns of implementation are the result of the interplay between many actors and are conditioned strongly by context. (As has been found elsewhere; see for instance Wilkinson, 1983; Hartman *et al.*, 1983; Clark *et al.*, 1984).

IT and senior executives

An important group within the web of interests must be directors and senior executives. IT is publicized as a crucial matter for companies, so how involved were this group with the technology and its implementation? In each case senior executives were obviously focused on key business matters, different for each, but generally in the areas of financial viability, product design, costs, market behaviour and people issues. None of these senior managers talked of an explicit strategy for IT; that is a laid down and understood plan for introducing hardware and processes. There has, of course, been wide discussion in the literature about the degree and extent of strategy definition and its several levels of creation and implementation (see for instance Hofer and Schendel's (1978) suggested composite of strategies). And it must be said that for every senior executive interviewed (with the sole exception of the chairman of Fashion) there were always super-ordinate executives beyond the scope of the research who were influencing matters.

Nevertheless the overriding impression was that the interviewed senior personnel did not seem especially knowledgeable about, or interested in, the information technologies in improving organizational effectiveness. Nor, with some exceptions, were these executives giving strong leadership in the evolving IT-led changes associated with IT. This is confirmation of a report by P.E. Consulting Services (1986) on attitudes and acceptance of IT and anticipated by Dearden (1983).

Throughout the upper ranks of all the companies there was seldom an enthusiasm for IT matching the supposed importance of the technologies registered in the media. Most of the senior executives had viewed IT as 'main-frame computing' with important but limited scope for reducing manpower and thus cost in specific shop-floor and clerical procedures. 'Our first mistake was regarding the computer as a glorified accounting machine' (E-13) sums up this attitude.

In only one company (Hardwear) was a director responsible solely for management information systems, and even there engineering applications were not within his province. Only in Components did it appear that the whole gamut of IT was being driven from some long-term and corporate plane, though this did not seem to include organizational design or management development in relation to IT.

Senior managers were aware of the technologies, but often only in a general way. Certainly they rarely had detailed technical knowledge. Managers at lower levels plainly regarded IT implementation as a matter of tactics. This was especially so at Fashion and Integral where absence of a plan was joked about. In all the companies senior executives were predominantly reacting to technological specialists. Confirmation of this comes from the Butler Cox (1986) report, which concludes that top management is too willing to regard an 'IT strategy' as a chore to be delegated to the systems department.

IT and middle managers

The main dialectic to initiate decisions to install IT systems was between MIS (middle) managers and their supporting enthusiasts among functional managers and directors. The discussions appear generally to be asymmetrical due to the extreme differences in knowledge of IT and its potential between the 'designers' (MIS for instance) and senior executives.

Accounting disciplines were widely quoted as acting against introduction of the technology. Proving, by cost-benefit analysis, the advantage of a proposed application was commonly regarded as difficult. While the costs could be estimated easily, the benefits were problematic. Outcomes such as use of released floor space, better quality or reliability of the product or service, new learning by managers, are often impossible to bring into the equation. Kaplan (1986b) comes to similar conclusions regarding computer-integrated manufacturing.

There is a certain inevitability of events as the costs of hardware (computer, automation and telecommunication) continue to fall rapidly. Cost-benefit analyses are thus seen to be moving unerringly in favour of technology-based processes. It is ironic that while cost-benefit analyses are often quoted as evidence for *not* introducing technology, post-event analyses are seldom made in any of the companies. Thus there is no accumulation of rigorous data either in favour, or against, IT.

The web of organizational forces surrounding IT is convoluted. Certainly the tensions presented in the literature (Friedman, 1985 and Markus, 1983 for instance) between systems designers and systems users were found in all five companies. But the detail in each case revealed many cross-currents.

Both the 'designers' and the 'users' are not discrete entities: rather each group contains many interests and enthusiasms. On the designer side the various aspects, or component technologies of IT, for instance office automation, plant engineering, telecommunications, software acquisition, are seldom coordinated. In no case was there an overall responsibility for these elements, and often communication between these several interests was poor. Examples of antagonism and competition between factions of the designers were quoted often.

Nevertheless, expertise of computing and IT-based systems lay overwhelmingly with the designers, who were continually updating their knowledge through courses and contacts with hardware and software suppliers. This was in contrast to the user-managers who were generally poorly informed on the technologies. But from the viewpoint of most managers there was another distinction. Designers (both in MIS and in plant automation functions) were seen as lacking in understanding of management and organizational processes, not least of the personnel dimension. This confirms findings in the literature, for instance Mumford and Henshall (1978); Mumford (1981); Collins (1983 and 1984); Wynne and Otway (1982); and Newman and Rosenberg (1985). All these point to designers relying on deterministic-rationalistic models of managerial behaviour and lacking awareness of management practicalities. In both the Butler Cox report (1986) and the Eosys report (1986) executives express disappointment and frustration with MIS departments, and the kinds of IT systems they are designing.

Another aspect considered important here was the absence of liaison between system designers and the Personnel function. Nor was there any indication anywhere that organization–design was taking into account the possible, or even the desired, structural or process implications of IT. For instance, specific training or preparation of managers for IT was rare.

Many operating managers spoke of the 'distance' between the pro-posers of change, often MIS, and themselves. They were virtually sub-merged in day-to-day detail management and with little understanding of the technologies were at considerable disadvantage in debates with the designers and in IT implementation. With the exception of Com-ponents, there was a widespread conservatism among user-managers. Pressure to maintain the status quo was strong, and evidence of counter-implementation was often apparent. Managers maintained low personal visibility or were reluctant to adopt new systems. Systems experts were cast as 'over-clever'; systems were characterized as confus-ing or not useful. (In fact, a corroboration of the list of counter-implementation techniques given by Keen, 1981.) Indeed, the reluctance of British managers to take on new responsibilities has been identified by Swords-Isherwood and Senker (1978) as a major cause of Britain's poor performance in innovation. The designers often used 'counter-counter-implementation' approaches such as seconding systems special-ists to work alongside line managers, that is becoming 'insiders', to assist introduction of new routines or different technology.

Overall, in spite of many problems, technology is spreading. Middle managers are gradually becoming more IT-knowledgeable, and their attitudes are slowly turning in favour of the technologies. What this research shows particularly is the web of interests associated with IT. To say managers have choices in the use of IT (see for instance Buchanan, 1982, and Hartman *et al.*, 1983), is true. But the cases here reveal the many divergent interests, and levels of understanding of IT and its effects, among managers. The actual IT outcome in the short term is contingent upon several situational factors and not least upon the ongoing dialectic at middle-management levels.

Imperatives in IT implementation

The revealed pattern of implementation and usage was highly differenti-ated between companies and between organizational functions. With little company-wide overview of IT at senior levels, the exact anatomy of IT applications resulted from particular enthusiasms and technical knowledge of managers and their perceived potential for favourable outcomes. What often appeared to be lacking was the ability to syn-thesize IT expertise, and experience of the 'on-the-ground' management context.

IT enthusiasts were also faced with a massive momentum to maintain the status quo (except at Components) and extreme difficulties of bridging the gap in understanding of IT and its potential between themselves and user-managers. In fact abilities in creating and maintain-ing bridges appear to be crucial. Speed and effectiveness of IT diffusion was often dependent on key individuals (usually managers). This confirms the oft-quoted observation that 'champions' are of critical importance in the introduction of new practices (see Buchanan in Winch (ed.), 1983).

However, each organizational function seems to have its own IT character. Computer-aided-design (except at Fashion) has been established for a decade, and basic financial systems for much longer. Personnel departments, on the other hand, in four companies were virtually untouched by IT. And, again except at Components, manufacturing managers seem to have been the slowest to be convinced of the advantages of IT. In spite of the patchy and often paradoxical patterns of IT use, it seems there is an underlying logic. Implementation is being driven by six separate but interlocking imperatives. These are sketched in Figure 5.1.

For clarity in the following analysis, the characterization of IT usage in chapter two, is repeated here:

1. the management information system (MIS) part of the management data processes. This in turn can be divided into two forms:
   a. *transaction processing*—the systematized electronic processing of standardized elements of data, for instance, wages preparation;
   b. *decision support* for control, coordination and planning at any organizational level and with any time horizon. Decision support may be a derivative of transaction processing—that is an automatic, planned outcome in terms of useful management indices; or it may be electronic processing of data relatively separate from the generality of operational transactions. In the latter case, func-

---

1. With time: increasing distribution of access to computer facilities.

2. With time: paper–manual systems decreasing; IT systems increasing; as a proportion of all systems.

3. With time: focus on cost reduction effect of IT reducing; focus on added value effect of IT increasing.

4. With time: emphasis on transactions processing decreasing; emphasis on decision support increasing.

5. With time: IT facilities and applications ascending organizational hierarchy from shop floor and office-floor transactions, through operations control, through tactical planning and control, to strategic planning and control.

6. With time: integration of systems is increasing; number of separate systems is decreasing.

Figure 5.1 'Imperatives' in IT implementation within organizations

tional managers commonly have autonomy of access to data and the computer operations (that is independent of MIS).

2. organizational communications—again in two forms:
   a. as *electronic mail*, e-mail, which offers an alternative to face-to-face oral, telephone, and telex arrangements between people within the organization or between them and people in other organizations.
   b. as *networks* of terminals with rapid access to data banks. In this mode people are accessing stored information at various levels of derivation from the original data; there may be communication between people and the system, or between computers, and
3. control engineering—that is those data processes associated with control of machine-accomplished physical activities such as machining or assembly on the shop floor. These control processes may be integrated with other information systems in the organization. Control engineering is not included in this study.

This categorization is regarded as important and in what follows will be referred to as:

- Transaction processing
- Decision support
- E-mail
- Networking, and
- Control engineering and automation (on the shop-floor).

'Transaction processing', that is repetitive, usually low-complexity data procedures have historically been carried out by large groups of clerical unskilled or semi-skilled staff. High volumes of transaction processing occur in certain functions such as accounting (payroll, billing, costing, ledgers) and in inventory control (purchasing, warehousing). But it also occurs (depending on the company) in other functions such as production (production control, quality control, product specification, standards and assembly routing). Each function has therefore a specific amount, and degree of complexity, of transaction processing. Most of this has traditionally been handled by the 'serried' ranks of clerical workers at the lower-middle of the hypothetical organizational pyramid.

Computerization is carried out most easily where there are high volumes of low-complexity transactions. And the incentive to management to reduce transaction cost through reduction in numbers of clerical workers (and this means increase in productivity) was especially visible in these tasks. Thus as Nolan has argued, the initial motivation for IT applications is cost reduction and takes place at these 'low' organizational levels. As computerization moves sequentially (but in a largely unplanned manner) up the pyramid, volumes of transactions decrease, transaction complexity increases and the potential for labour cost reduction is less.

Early computer-driven transaction processing was facilitated by hardware operation speed, by the relative ease of constructing software and by inputting practices being straightforward. The greater difficulties of more complex transactions are increasingly offset by the continuing increase in hardware speed, by more effective later generation software and the improvement in telecommunications and display facilities.

The continuing and rapid reduction in cost per performance is driving the spread of terminals, personal computers, printers and shop-floor automation. As hardware costs continue to fall the distribution of *access* to IT-driven systems is increasing in all the companies. The spectrum of IT usage, from Fashion, where there was only one personal computer in use and few managers had terminals, to Components at which microcomputers and terminals were commonplace, is wide indeed. But in both, the extension of IT use is continuing.

Transaction processing by main-frame computer produces management indices which are useful to operations planning and control—and have been so used in all the companies for years. 'Decision support' for managers, using independent personal computers and giving autonomy over data and computer packages has, since 1980, been spreading rapidly in all companies except Fashion. By and large improved decision support is an 'added-value', rather than a 'cost reduction', imperative. However, these two imperatives in respect of decision support for managers are often inseparable. Better and faster decisions are an important constituent of manager productivity and despite added value often have cost reduction consequences also. Combination of personal computers and their access to main-frame networks is allowing managers to 'down-load' centrally available data and then to have autonomy over data manipulation. This sophistication redresses the balance of data ownership in favour of user-managers.

Thus now in all the companies both cost-reduction and added-value imperatives are operating simultaneously. Further, the reducing cost of hardware is driving spread of access. As repeatedly shown in this study several IT tendencies impinge on an organizational situation at the same time, making cost-benefit analyses extraordinarily difficult. In fact although the idea of such analyses were often introduced by interviewed managers the practice of post-event analysis is rare.

One other conclusion, considered significant here, is that as paper–manual (PM) systems, or earlier IT-based systems are replaced by later IT systems, there is usually a reduction in data redundancy and a coalescence of sub-systems. The total number of sub-systems is thus reducing with time. The integration of data systems which this implies transcends organizational responsibility structures.

In summary, this research reveals the spread and use of IT to be weakly coordinated, with many groups of managers taking part in the unrolling debate, decisions and implementation. Certainly the twin Nolan forces—for cost reduction and for added value—are prime, but the spread of access is itself a positive feedback in the acceleration of IT use. It would seem that the inherent characteristics of IT are driving organizations and their management inevitably toward higher levels of technology usage, productivity and systematization. However, and importantly, it is inescapably seen that the nature of the developing new practices is strongly conditioned by the existing culture in each company.

Implications for managers

Preface

As the literature establishes, technology has always been a powerful agent for change, both in society generally and in work. The definition of technology is not easy, and variations in definition undoubtedly give rise to problems in assessing conclusions of researchers. The common-place view is that technology equates with artefacts, and more usually in today's world with machines. The symbol T^m will be used here for this interpretation. But as Schumpeter (1939) pointed out, technology may be regarded as including knowledge, concepts and practices as well as hardware. While this may be valid, and indeed may offer conceptual advantages, such a wide definition leads to extraordinary difficulties in identifying and separating technological effects. This wider definition will be given the symbol T^+ here.

Until recently, technology (T^m) has been primarily either within the product (for instance in cars, pumps, washing machines) or has been a substitution of 'machinery' for human effort and skills within the arena of *physical* processes. Its applications were thus mostly on the shop floor and its effects mainly for labour processes. Historically, increasing technology in both products and in production did have some concomitant implications for the work of managers, as is indicated in chapter two. However, the literature broadly implies that such technological applications were of no great consequence for management process.

Now the essential difference with information technology is that it is just that: technology applied to information processes. Although it has physical manifestations and consequences, it is within the arena of organizational 'intelligence' systems, discussed in chapter two, that IT is making its principal direct impact. IT is increasing the effectiveness of the total organization to process data. From this simple but profound concept the whole range of implications of IT flows.

It is clear from the field work that this increased data processing effectiveness of IT can be conceptualized as resulting from three vectors:

- the Technology Vector (Tv)
- the Systems Vector (Sv)
- the Productivity Vector (Pv)

These vectors operate simultaneously and in practice are highly inter-woven. Nevertheless, this conceptual framework (see Figure 5.2) is useful in throwing light on the implications of IT on managers' work and is discussed here briefly.

As Beer emphasizes throughout his writings, an organization can always be considered as a system and its various activities as linked sub-systems. But there is a range of 'hardness' of systems ranging from the hard control systems of a computer-managed machine, through less-hard accounting systems, to 'soft' social systems. There is a parallel degree of deliberate intention in the design of such systems. In the harder cases of engineering and accounting the systems are carefully designed, whereas social systems tend to evolve in a largely undesigned way. Of course certain organizational factors such as structure and training are important for the emergence of the social system specific to a particular company.

IT, deriving from its generic characteristics discussed in chapter two, increases the extent of, and sophistication of, intended and designed hard data systems. This is considered to be the systems vector (Sv).

It is possible to imagine that without the T^m of IT, that is using knowledge and concepts of data processing without the hardware, organizations might become increasingly systematized. But such non-technology (non-T^m) systems would suffer the inherent drawbacks of paper–manual (PM) arrangements, of which the greatest is probably slowness of operation. Pre-IT systems may operate at speeds slower than, and often much slower than, the 'actual' processes (of production, sales, decisions) they are associated with. IT offers specifically techno-logical characteristics of speed; large, fast memories; interconnectability and access; and others discussed in chapter two which, it is here suggested, can be seen as the technological vector (Tv). In other words, there are effects due to Tv which would not arise from systematization (Sv) alone. Specifically IT systems operate at speeds as fast as, and often faster than, the 'actual' processes (of production, sales, decisions) they are associated with. This change from pre-IT systems is profound.

Taken together Sv and Tv increase the effectiveness of data processing throughout the organization and thus increase productivity both in offices and on the shop floor. For a given output, numbers of people—both staff and management—fall, as will be discussed shortly. And from this productivity vector (Pv) derive many other consequences for managers.

Following the themes recurring in the literature the framework used in the field work and in the case presentations was:

IT vectors	Tv Sv Technology and systems vectors	Pv Productivity vector
Managers' work		
General character	Increases priority of data management; increases pace; decreases primacy of designatory structures; reduces differences between managerial and non-managerial work; increases need for flexibility; increases need for technological and systems skills in managers	Decreases amount of personnel administration for line managers; increases emphasis on team management
People issues	Reduces 'tiers'; reduces number of managers; changes labour skills; increases subordinate 'professionalism'	Reduces labour; decreases detail in personal administration; increased team developments
'Interpersonal' communication	Electronic mail increases organizational transparency; reduces 'linking-pin' primacy of managers	Reduces number of people in the interpersonal network
Information management	Increases data access; reduces data redundancy; increases system integration; increases data quantities; increases organizational transparency; increases system centralization	
Decision making	Increases decision support; increases relevancy and priority problems; increases 'sphere of visibility'; increases pressure to react; increases need for goal clarity	Reduces detail in personnel administration decisions

Figure 5.2 Paradigm of IT vectors and managers' work

- The character of managers' work
- Managers and people
- Managers and communication
- Managers and decision making

This format was found to represent well the actualities found in the companies and is used in this analysis.

The character of managers' work

Overwhelmingly, the descriptions of managers' work and roles in the literature is evident throughout the company studies. Characterizations of that work as weakly defined, highly fragmented—with many brief episodes and much interruption and attention switching—was shown to be the case in all the companies studied. Managers are usually involved in several tasks simultaneously and constantly moving between them as they reassess priorities. Streams of oral, written and telecommunicated data impinge on managers from all sides, stimulating reactions of communication or action. The typical 'action-orientation' of managers described by researchers was commonly observed. This basic nature of managers' work appears to be little changed by IT so far.

Another important conclusion is the variability of IT effects, for managers and for the organization generally. Information technology has many forms and is interacting with complex, and different, practices in each case. Thus the exact implications for each manager are unique. While the tendencies discussed here appear to be pushing the organizations in 'inevitable' directions, in the short run the prevailing cultures are powerful in conditioning the IT effects.

Managers are acutely aware of the greater rate of change in recent years. Competitive pressures and the consequent implications for products, pricing, productivity and organizational processes are much in their minds. But it is clear also that technology, and especially IT, is seen as a major transforming force on their company and on management. While the popular press, and IT vendors, have grossly under-estimated the time scale of IT consequences in organizations, managers widely anticipate radical changes in the longer term. It is axiomatic that managers are crucially implicated in these changes. Though it is not a new phenomenon, the 'management of change' is a key component in virtually all the work of the managers studied.

IT is rarely perceived as a single technology by managers: rather, they spoke of those technologies, and those effects of them, that were impinging in their own spheres. Production managers were concerned about automation, robotics and computer-driven production control, quality control and systems. Marketing managers were focused on analytical 'packages', on customer enquiry response systems and methods of updating sales people in the field using portable equipment and telephone coupling to office-based computers. The point is that while IT has a common technological basis, its plurality is important.

This plurality means that IT expertise is usually, and naturally, divided among several functions. In no company was a single executive responsible for the total IT arena. Yet IT systems are superceding traditional functional divisions: the organization is becoming a single integrated system. The transitions from the relatively 'separated' structure compartments toward this system entity provide difficulties for many managers with strongly functional perspectives.

BALANCE OF ATTENTION

Earlier three vectors were suggested: the technology vector (Tv), the systems vector (Sv) and the productivity vector (Pv). The technology and systems vectors of IT are intimately bound together—but they are different. Technology, in the sense of artefacts or machinery (T^m) has historically been applied primarily at the shop floor. Thus managers in that arena have long been involved in technological matters. And in all five companies IT is facilitating increased technology at the shop floor. Inevitably the technological component of these managers' jobs is steadily becoming larger.

Technology, as machinery, has been encroaching on office environments for many years (as telephones, telex, typewriters, copiers, etc). But essentially for decades, office practices and more importantly management practices have been little changed by this technology (T^m). In its wider form T^+, to include concepts and techniques, technology has always been a part of management. IT, neglecting for the moment its systems vector (Sv), brings an increase in both machinery (T^m) and in concepts and techniques to managers. The computer terminal and personal computer are becoming a standard part of office and management equipment as the telephone became years previously. But computer access is also bringing to managers techniques of analysis and data reformatting unavailable previously—a concept technology. This is interwoven with the systematization of data handling discussed earlier.

Management has thus been forced by IT to become both more technological and more systematized. Information management is demanding a different and higher order of attention from managers. Questions of systems design, modification and operation, decision support, data value and priority and the associated choices of application of hardware and software have moved to centre stage for managers.

In the past 'management of people' had been the prime, if not overwhelming, dimension of many managers' work. The relatively low-productivity regimes meant large numbers of people and that in turn produced an emphasis on personnel administration issues. Managers became focused upon, and at times submerged in, matters of industrial relations and social management. Planning for, coordinating and controlling large numbers of people consumed much management time and energy.

The productivity vector (Pv) of IT is arguably now beginning to move these companies into a 'virtuous spiral' of faster improvements in productivity and especially information management productivity and so reducing numbers of staff. The natural priority of 'social management' is therefore declining—or to continue the thespian metaphor—it is moving off centre stage.

THE ADAPTIVE MILIEU

Not one of the companies studied could be called 'typical'. Yet, except for Components, their cultures, structures and processes can perhaps be characterized as 'traditional' in the British context. This implies (the word 'relatively' is assumed in each case):

• Well-defined hierarchy
• Many hierarchical tiers
• High visibility of management authority and status
• Well-defined functions and departments
• Boundaries difficult to cross
• Low productivities in manufacturing processes
• Low productivities in information handling (office work)
• Large numbers of staff
• Large amounts of attention on people issues and 'social management'
• Except on shop floor, low 'technological' orientation of managers
• Low attention by managers to information management
• Low integration between sub-systems
• Low organizational transparency
• High specificity of data ownership
• Low definition and 'ownership' of company goals and policy

It is argued here that IT is tending to reverse all these characteristics and transforming organizations from 'traditional' to a different state which will be termed the 'adaptive milieu'.

Within the adaptive milieu there is less weight given to 'designatory' structures and more given to information management structures and processes. Because of the ubiquity of data access, stimulation to decision making and action is high. Thus managers are prompted to react quickly without time to consult upwards for guidance. Managers are therefore forced to decide autonomously which information to use, with whom to communicate and priorities of the moment. Previously designated rules, regulations and priorities based on the past become obsolete rapidly. As Beer (1975) points out 'only variety can absorb variety' (Ashby's law of requisite variety): 'It is the rise in technology which allows the variety of individual behaviour.' The individual middle manager is less guided by detailed rules and needs knowledge of and 'ownership' of company goals and policy so that he can react and proact in the most relevant way.

In a sense traditional organizations were based on strong designatory 'social' structures and processes, with weaker information structures and processes. The adaptive milieu reverses these, with the premium an *adaptation*. This is an extension from the 'organic' organization identified by Burns and Stalker as preferred in situations of fast change. IT creates tendencies which force, and allow, a high degree of adaptation and therefore call for qualities of creativity, initiative taking, flexibility and responsiveness of a much higher order than hitherto. Within the adaptive milieu team building based on relevance of communication patterns and relevance to task performance is prime and requires personnel management of a nature much different from that in traditional cultures. At Components this is the general situation, but small, professional, colleague-like teams were also found in the other companies.

Naturally there are strains between the culture, structure and processes aligned with the designatory-hierarchical-traditional orientation and the adaptive milieu which is emerging. There also exist tensions between those traditional patterns and the technological-systematic emphasis associated with increasing IT. Paradoxically, then, 'intelligence processes' are becoming more systematic, while interpersonal and social processes are becoming less so. As the spread and use of IT is proceeding in a largely patchy and somewhat uncoordinated manner, the topography of these transitions and tensions is convoluted.

MANAGEMENT WORK CHARACTER, AND HIERARCHY

Patently the character of management work has always been a function of tier position in the hierarchy. Junior managers are concerned mostly with shorter time horizons and the immediate control of personnel and tasks. As the management hierarchy is ascended, the focus moves increasingly to longer time scales and strategic planning and decisions. Undoubtedly this relationship of work and hierarchy continues.

Not surprisingly the implications of IT for managers are also hierarchy-related. It is at the middle and lower levels of the organization that the bulk transaction processes (of accounting, purchasing, inventory control) go on, and where the IT systematization is most applied. First- and second-line managers are most aware of the labour reductions, labour skill changes and the immediate sub-system effects, especially transparency and increased vulnerability.

It is at middle levels of the hierarchy that managers are most IT-involved. For there, computer-produced analyses are widely available; but also such managers are often using personal computers. User-designer debates on priorities and details of applications and the transition issues from pre-IT systems are worked out at these levels also.

At the highest levels, executives have often received computer printouts for some years, though such data is gradually becoming more sophisticated, timely and useful. Personal computers are rarely used by these senior managers, though. Indeed such managers are somewhat insulated from the direct effects of IT, and this may partially account for their apparent lack of leadership in IT acquisition and development. The field work confirmed the oft-repeated findings that top managers are not well informed on or especially enthusiastic about the application of new technology.

Managers and people

The improvement in the effectiveness of information management creates the 'productivity vector' (Pv) introduced earlier. IT is thus manifestly reducing labour content per output in all five companies. It has not been possible to evince clear correlations between IT application and numbers of people for several reasons. First, this research is not a longitudinal study and numbers of staff quoted by managers were impossible to validate especially for past years. Also, in each company there were ongoing changes of staff in departments, and overall, related to various current issues. In addition, changes of structure and titles add further uncertainty. The reasons for lack of clarity were not always logistical: managers were evidently cautious in quoting specifics in the politically sensitive arena of reducing employment associated with new technologies.

Also, the impression was gained from managers, that notwithstanding some warmth towards IT, they defended the need to hold their levels of labour. This is not surprising as managerial status is in some measure related to numbers of subordinates. The consequence is that there is probably a lag in labour reduction in relation to the take-up of IT.

Nevertheless, in all five companies there was a general acceptance among managers that IT displaces staff. This productivity vector comprises several components:

- direct substitution of IT-driven processes and equipment, on the shop floor and in offices, for the effort and skills of people;
- reduction of data and system redundancy, eliminating some tasks altogether;

- secondary reductions in tasks consequent upon reduction in numbers of personnel (for instance in personnel departments, in cleaning and in refectories);
- reductions in 'tiers' in the hierarchy partly related to labour reduction and partly to organizational transparency.

The reduced need for intermediate managers was often mentioned and confirms the findings of Barras and Swann (1983) in the insurance industry. Child (1984) and Rothwell (1984) come to similar conclusions. This is in direct contrast with the pre-IT literature which even as late as 1977 (Argyris) was lauding the importance of middle management in interpreting data for senior executives. In the research here the tendency toward flatter hierarchies was frequently mentioned though managers also said number of tiers were unchanged in recent years. This may again be a case of personnel and structural changes lagging behind events. There are echoes here of Dawson and McLoughlin's (1984) study of computerization of railway freight movements. They suggest that the new communication channels provided by the computer obviated the need for hierarchical reporting. One layer of management, in consequence, was expected to 'wither on the vine' as direct restructuring was frustrated by middle management.

There are also other non-direct effects of IT which tend to reduce staff. Patently, the physical size of electronic components, and thus of assemblies, is reducing (see chapter two). Production managers frequently referred to equipment which a few years previously was the size of a filing cabinet and now was a single integrated circuit card. Thus the space needed in production facilities per throughput is decreasing. This decreased volume per performance also was quoted in the applications of the equipment. It would seem therefore that the space required for a given turnover or output is decreasing.

A similar effect is created by reduction of system redundancy. Engineering design and manufacturing planning are now carried out centrally at all four engineering companies and transmitted electronically to relevant departments. Similarly, at Integral, fault diagnosis of customers' equipment is taking place electronically over telephone lines. These activities naturally have tended to reduce staff and space.

It seems inescapable that the 'traditional' low-technology, low-productivity organizations, which meant large numbers of people, and which itself created demands for more support and management roles, is now in reverse. IT in the companies studied is causing an upward trend in productivity, a downward trend in staff numbers.

The numbers of staff reporting to first-line supervisors was only marginally down overall. However, generally, managers more involved with IT (the 'A' and 'B/C' groups) reported greater reductions of staff (see Appendix 2) responsible to their first-line supervisors. Also there were several examples of small teams of professionals highly involved in IT systems.

The skills of workers were not studied but managers commonly introduced this topic. In their perceptions, as the lower complexity transactions were computerized, unskilled and semi-skilled jobs disappear—in offices, warehouses and on the shop floor. The work then associated with IT-driven systems was usually seen as requiring 'higher' skills—especially calling for understanding the data system, initiative taking and independent thought.

Definition and classification of 'skills' is seldom easy, and this is especially so for mental and social skills. Paper transactions at lower levels of complexity are usually repetitive and require carrying out relatively explicit sequences of simple listing, matching, validating and filing activities. As these routines are absorbed into machine systems, the work that remains appears to be more 'management-like'. That is to say, the work is less definable and calls for workers to take more initiatives.

A simple example of this is in word processing (widespread in all the companies), which reduces the need for perfect first-time keyboarding (an 'old' skill of a routine type) and increases opportunities for creative layout (a new 'initiative' skill). Much of the early literature (Buchanan and Boddy, 1982; and Crompton and Reid, 1983) finds that technology produces deskilling of clerical work. Managers in the research here often held the opposite view.

Managers also commonly believed that the access of their 'immediate' subordinates to information available to themselves is increasing. The increased access to the network, including electronic mail, has another important effect: it increases the expectation of rapid response. This in turn reduces the time available for upward consulting by staff, increasing autonomy at lower levels. When increased access is added to the perceived increase in autonomy and initiative-taking of subordinates, the effect seems to be to reduce the differences between managerial and non-managerial work. (Rothwell, 1984, also noted this.) A good example of this is the distribution department at Hardwear in which every staff member has a VDU and can call up a variety of data on product availability, product specifications, price and discounts. The telephone transactions with customers are carried out with rare references to the office manager (who in fact has no better information than his staff).

While there is wide variability in functions and departments, the persistent impression among managers is that the number of people for which they are responsible is decreasing and the average skill and professional competence is increasing. Overall, reduced number of subordinates at any level must mean a reduction in 'personnel administration' in matters of absenteeism, tardiness, health and safety and records. The tendency upwards of increased access, autonomy and initiative-taking, coupled with greater skills and qualifications is probably slowly changing the subordinate–superordinate relationships away from primary hierarchical, and towards a 'team', culture. This has already been discussed under 'general character of managers' work. A summary of IT tendencies for 'people' issues is shown below.

IT tendencies for 'people' issues:
- Reducing staffing due to direct IT applications
- Reducing staffing due to indirect effects (such as reducing system redundancy, and needed space)
- Reducing number of tiers and intermediary managers
- Increasing skills and qualifications of staff
- Increasing staff access at lower levels
- Increasing autonomy and initiative taking by staff
- Away from hierarchical and toward a 'team' culture

Managers and communication

As introduced in chapter two much that happens in organizations is concerned with communication, which is dealt with in this analysis under two headings: first information management, that is data capture, analysis, transmission (and other data mechanisms) of a 'designed' nature—for instance an accounting system; second, interpersonal communication, which has a more informal, undesigned, 'social' nature.

INFORMATION MANAGEMENT

It is the increasing effectiveness in information management that IT confers which creates the major consequences for managers. The 'tendencies' produced by IT on this arena are summarized below.

IT tendencies for communication:
- Information management increasing in importance
- Increasing integration of sub-systems
- Increasing organizational transparency
- Increasing perception of data quantities
- Increased priority of data structures
- Increased perception of pace
- Increased reactivity
- Increased problems of data relevance and priority
- Increased feelings of vulnerability
- Little electronic mail used (except at Components), but increasing

- Where e-mail used extensively, initiative-taking and boundary-crossing increased
- Reducing data redundancy
- Reducing redundancy of sub-systems
- Reducing number of sub-systems
- Reducing specificity of data ownership
- Decreased priority of 'designatory' structures
- Movement towards real-time processes

INCREASING IMPORTANCE OF INFORMATION MANAGEMENT

Among the managers studied the time spent on systems design or modification or directly using terminals ranged from 1 to 13.6 hours per week. Details are shown in Figure 5.3. This evidence is backed up by comments from most managers that computing and systems are a much greater component of their work than five years previously. Receiving computer print-outs is commonplace on all manner of subjects; inputting data directly onto terminals, or querying data bases via terminals, equally so. Personal computers are spreading widely and in many instances used regularly in decision support.

Per Manager	Engineering		Hardwear		Fashion		Integral		Components	
	B/C	D	B/C	D	B/C	D	B/C	D	B/C	D
a. Has VDU in own office	.1	0	.4	0	1.0	.2	.8	.5	.6	.3
b. Has PC in own office	.2	.1	.2	0	0	0	0	0	.4	.1
c. No. of packages used	2.1	.4	1.8	.2	.6	.6	2.0	.2	1.9	.2
d. Hrs/week on systems design or modification	12.1	1.1	3.1	.8	2.8	.9	1.5	.9	1.6	.8
e. Hrs/week on terminals	1.5	0	4.9	.2	5.3	.5	8.3	.7	5	.3
f. E-mail messages per day	.2	.1	.7	0	0	0	.4	.2	8.3	9.6

Figure 5.3 Comparison of IT involvement

It is an inescapable conclusion that these management activities were not taking place some years earlier—perhaps five to twenty years depending on the company. Such activities are replacing other work then carried out by managers. In the companies studied, early IT systems were an overlay of pre-existent PM processes, as suggested by Hedberg (1980). As the experience of IT in the companies increased, there was an ever-increasing conversion of PM transactions into IT-driven processes.

INTEGRATION AND ORGANIZATIONAL TRANSPARENCY

Prior to the spread of computerization, organizational functions and departments had their own 'paper–manual' systems, often designed without strong overall company coordination. Each of these essentially separate sub-systems, limited in extent by 'designatory' structures, for instance department boundaries, and by lack of technical facilities, had their own data files. Thus there is in such cases a high degree of separation of sub-systems and files, and a low level and coordination of data and systems. As PM routines are increasingly converted to IT-driven systems there is generally a reduction in data redundancy, a reduction in sub-system redundancy and an increase in 'tightness' of systems in terms of timing, format, routing, access and synchronization. Sub-systems are absorbed into more wide-ranging systems: the number of discrete sub-systems reduces. This integration effect of IT has been noted by Nolan (1979), Barras and Swann (1983), Winch (1983), Bessant (1983) and Rajan Amin (1985).

Integration appears to develop as follows:

Stage 1 Extant sub-systems (say) A, B and C (which may be 'paper–manual' or earlier form of computer system).
Stage 2 System analysis and design consultations and planning, while A, B and C continue.
Stage 3 New system I installed incorporating A, B and C, resulting in:
  • strong designed-in coherence of A, B and C;
  • reduction in staff;
  • less direct managerial coordination between A, B and C required by managers;
  • less direct personnel administration (due to less staff) by managers;
  • reduction of data redundancy within A, B and C.
Stage 4 A, B and C sub-systems vanish.
Stage 5 I seen as single sub-system being considered for integration with similar sub-systems, II and III.

As sub-systems A, B and C transform to I, the system effects may be rapid: the new system comes on-stream immediately. Although characteristically de-bugging of the new system can take weeks and even months in difficult cases. However, some effects are sudden: several examples were found of immediate reductions in personnel and changes in working procedures. Whereas managers had often had some control over the design and operation of PM sub-systems, and over relevant data files, 'the design and control of the more sophisticated IT-driven systems are moving away from them. Design responsibility, even when there is consultation with operating managers, is with a central 'management information systems' staff. Much of the original system management (of A, B and C) is built into the system I itself. There is then a decreasing net amount of management (by people) as integration proceeds. The reduction of sub-systems, and integration between them, was widely seen as reducing the 'fuzziness' of the organization, especially across department or functional boundaries. A detailed example of this rationalizing process at Engineering is shown in Figure 5.4. Clearly the extent and importance of information management is increasing, and especially so since 1981.

Date	Computerized transactions	Millions of instructions per second (MIPS)	On-line terminals
1960–7	Payroll, general ledger		(batch entry)
1968–73	Above plus material and production control; engineering and personnel records		(batch entry)
1974–8		1.5	(batch entry)
1979–80		2	25
1981			100
1982			400
1984	Above plus engineering design; manufacturing assembly; acounting/costing; dealer voice response; order data; purchasing	40	600

Figure 5.4 Accelerating expansion of IT at Engineering

Traditionally, organizational structures (designatory structures) have been based on relatively 'autonomous' functions (such as marketing). Happenings within these units were largely contained within their own cultures and systems and 'intelligence' about them was transmitted by unit managers after suitable filtering. In this transmission of information managers acted (and still act) as a 'linking-pin' (Likert, 1961).

As systems become integrated, indices useful in work monitoring, or for decision making, are automatically produced and transmitted across boundaries. Not only is such information moving across functional boundaries, it is accessible (to anyone with authority to access it) up the hierarchy. At Fashion for instance, a director with a terminal in his office monitors operator efficiency—information automatically derived from production control systems. It is thus more difficult for managers to conceal the immediate reality from their super-ordinates. As Burns *et al.* (undated) found in coal mining, this process increases supervision and control by senior managers as they gain information instantaneously with the local managers. The elimination of, or at least reduction in, intermediate 'linking-pins' in information transactions in reducing delays between actions and knowledge of those actions being widely available. Also, as many managers said, the actualities are concealed with difficulty.

This loss of 'ownership' and control of data, coupled with increased organizational transparency, is frequently perceived by managers as increasing their vulnerability. Another associated feature comes from the opposite direction: their subordinates are now often able to access data as easily and quickly as the managers. In fact in some circumstances, especially where managers are not terminal-skilled, subordinates have better access than their managers. IT systems thus increase the 'sphere of visibility' of users, both managers and non-managers.

The increase in spheres of visibility, the reduction of the primacy of functional boundaries and the movement toward 'real time' are all factors improving the understanding of middle and senior managers of activities in the 'lower' reaches of the organization. This then is changing the balance of power—away from supervisors and junior managers.

It has to be emphasized that the degree of corporate-level planning of computer-based systems was found to vary greatly. Thus the advantages of reducing data redundancy, and of integrating sub-systems were, as yet, being achieved only in the more experienced and sophisticated situations. At Fashion there was no coordination of hardware, software or data systems between the two computer centres and thus no integration. On the other hand at Engineering an overview computerization committee had been in existence for years, and undoubtedly integration and coalescence of sub-systems were coming. Though even there, complaints of 'lack of coordination' were frequent from managers.

However, in each company, there was a definite trend towards greater corporate overview of systematization with an anticipation amongst managers that numbers of systems will diminish as will data and system redundancy. (See for example, the integrated manufacturing system expected at Hardwear, which will integrate production scheduling, inventory control, purchasing, engineering specification and control of production equipment.)

This indicates an increased centralization of design and operation of systems. Indeed, whereas previously PM arrangements were to an extent limited by responsibility boundaries, and thus under some control of local managers, computer systems are not. Because of the current sophistication of software, the available size of data bases and the widespread access to terminals in the more advanced companies, IT systems transcend responsibility or functional boundaries.

This increasing overview of computerization applies especially to transaction processing, which is characterized by repetitive data processes amenable to definition in terms of format, timing and routing, for instance accounting.

DATA QUANTITY AND RELEVANCE

Although electronic transactions are increasing in volume in all five companies, and although such transactions are patently absorbing paper systems, managers commonly complained that the amount of paper is increasing. It seems that as more printers, copiers and faster printers become widely available, paper output increases. MIS specialists thought this would be an intermediate phase, and that paper would eventually decrease, as VDUs increased in distribution. However, managers are as yet not sufficiently experienced in terminal use to do without the convenience, and security to themselves, of having paper records at hand.

Managers usually perceived the *quantity* of data available to be increasing which is probably related to several factors. First, there is the increase in amounts of paper mentioned above. But in addition there is the increased *distribution* of data, because of the increased terminal access, and increased organizational transparency. A consequence of this data overload is problems of priority and data relevancy which many managers felt and which were undoubtedly acute in Components, the most advanced IT user. These issues are treated under decision making, to follow.

INTERPERSONAL COMMUNICATION

Interpersonal communication, in all five companies, remains at the heart of management processes. Talking with subordinates was everywhere regarded as of high importance by the surveyed managers. Similarly the whole panoply of consultation among managers continues. The only direct application of IT in this arena is in electronic messaging (e-mail). All the evidence suggests that in each company the patterns of inter-personal communication are deeply embedded within the culture, and as yet, are little changed by e-mail.

E-mail is used at Components about 100 times as much per manager as in the other companies, though of course this is partly because of the higher availability of terminals. But at Components the culture is highly favourable towards initiative-taking and flexible and experimental approaches by its staff who are therefore less constrained by 'desig-natory' structures than their equivalents in the other companies. The extensive e-mail usage therefore grows out of that culture and is con-tinually reinforced by it. In the other companies the cultures, though all different, tend to be less positive toward initiative-taking, and especially toward boundary-crossing and experimentalism, and in each e-mail is little utilized. This even applies at Integral where the technology is well understood and terminals widely available.

The sources of change in interpersonal communication relating to IT derive from its effects on information management and on decision making (the systems and technology vectors) and in reducing and upskilling staff (the productivity vector).

Oral communication still appears to be a dominant management behaviour. Managers claimed their (mostly oral) consultations with subordinates, peers and superordinates had increased in recent years. There was no change in numbers of 'meetings'. Even allowing for wishful thinking, all the survey and interview material tends to show an increased importance given to interpersonal relationships generally.

Managers and decision making

Managers generally found this area the most difficult to recall and to disaggregate. Patently, decision making, as many researchers have found, is an amalgam of 'negotiations, habit, rule of thumb and muddling through' (Keen, 1981); quantified analysis of data is a minor contributor. However, the prevalent opinion in this research was that decisions are becoming more difficult and more complex. The current market climate was undoubtedly seen as the principal reason for these difficulties. Certain characteristics of increasing IT also appear to in-crease managers' perceptions of complexity.

IT tendencies for decision making:
- Increasing transaction processing (that is systematic communication) incorporates some decisions in programs, that is 'minor' decisions automated;

- Increased computer support in decision making;
- Increasing organization transparency leading to increased manager vulnerability;
- Increasing perceptions of decision complexity;
- Increasing decision prompting and manager reactivity;
- Manager perceptions of greater data quantity—problems of priority and relevance;
- Increasing data structure priority;
- Increased 'pace';
- Increased need for goal/objectives structures;
- Integration of sub-systems allows automation verification of some decision data;
- Movement toward 'real' time;
- Reduced data redundancy and 'clearer' data;
- Decreasing organization structure primacy.

In approaching decisions, increased organizational transparency allows managers to draw relevant data from many sources, including from across functional boundaries. Similarly, post-decision consequences emerge rapidly from those sources, often automatically. Computer-derived management indices starkly point out results to an extensive audience. And, as previous sections have shown, with time, a greater proportion of the company's operations are falling into the systems net.

Computer aids to decision making are increasing in all companies. Computer print-outs giving comparisons of results over time, or against objectives, are ubiquitous. Managers in many functions quoted their use of such data—in production, quality control, marketing, warehousing, distribution, personnel and others. In its most advanced form, in Components, such information is used in virtually every decision and every discussion. Specific 'decision support' by computer 'packages', for instance in decision 'modelling', is also spreading, though is still a minor contribution to decisions. However in Components such support is commonly available to managers. Aids like this are usually welcomed by managers, who claim they reduce delays in decision making and improve decision quality.

As has been often mentioned here, managers commonly associate IT with increase in 'pace' of their work. This seems partly a communication factor, that is data is available faster, and partly a decision-prompting phenomenon. As Components is by far the most sophisticated IT regime, it may indicate the kinds of future likely to develop in other companies. A rich network of terminals exists for most managers and many non-managers—indeed an office without a terminal is unusual. Accessing the network for data, and for derived indices, is done continuously by most staff and managers. In addition, electronic mail is used about 100 times more often than in the other four companies. Managers are thus being prompted by this network for decisions, or for action, at a very high frequency. This accords well with a culture which acclaims fast response and is accepted as 'normal' or even 'favourable'.

In contrast, at Integral in spite of also being an advanced technology company, the IT network was very much less used in management decision support. Also, although there were problems of 'isolation' between sites, electronic mail was hardly used at all: evidence, it is suggested, of the critical role of the prevailing culture in influencing IT use.

Managers generally saw IT as improving their decisions—even in less sophisticated environments such as at Fashion. Usually that perceived improvement is associated with speed of data being available. It is postulated that several processes are again implicated. Time delays between an event in any function, and data on that event being available, are being shortened substantially by IT. In some circumstances instantaneous data is available. Also time delays between decisions and their being received at the operational point are also diminishing. Further, the traditional 'linking-pin' managerial mode in which information was passed up and down the hierarchy, and modified in the passing, is being replaced by more direct systems. It is suggested that all this gives managers a more immediate, and probably, a more real view of events: hence, the perceptions of IT improving decisions among managers.

As discussed earlier, IT is also tending to reduce definition of roles, both managerial and non-managerial. The primacy of 'designatory' structures, and conformity to 'traditional' communication patterns, is decreasing. In this regard, managers often expressed feelings of uncertainty. Again, this is to be expected. In companies of a 'traditional' type, such as Engineering and Hardwear, organizational structures—boundaries and hierarchy—were well defined and slow in changing. While this may have created some disadvantages for the company in terms of reduced initiative-taking, it did confer the advantage of giving security and confidence to managerial staff.

In Components, in every way different from the other four companies, there seems never to have been a solid structure. Rather that company has always been a dynamic, flexible and responsive organization. The effects of IT thus are resonant with the inherent culture and reinforce it. Components also has two important mechanisms not apparent in the other companies. First, there is a strong regime of forward planning, monitored and guided by computer. This forces managers to create plans and budgets for a long time scale ahead and to update these annually by prescribed dates. Second, consensus on future company directions and policies is sound: managers have a high confidence in the framework against which they take decisions. Both these mechanisms appear to provide managers with a stout knowledge base and to imbue the whole managerial corpus with resilience and positivity. Naturally these qualities derive from the whole culture and not only from the two mechanisms mentioned. In any event, the longstanding conventional structures in the 'traditional' organizations are being weakened and as yet are not being replaced by the Components-type mechanisms. The consequence is increased uncertainty for managers in these situations.

As has been noted, IT is reducing numbers of staff and probably increasing staff autonomy. It is therefore postulated here that managers are less called upon to take many minor decisions on personnel administration matters. The decision 'clutter' of these subjects is decreasing and managers are released, to an extent, to focus on matters of longer time scale and of greater weight. In fact, surveyed managers commonly reported that strategic and planning elements in their jobs were increasing as was the time horizon ahead on which they were focusing.

In all five companies then, IT is gradually extending its influence and creating many implications for the work and roles of managers. Chapter six sets out the conclusions from the research and reflections on their relevance to management and management development.

6 Conclusions and reflections

I have an increased horizon with regard to information—rapid data movement is paramount; my job is more and more about managing data and decisions. I ask myself with less people—what is a manager? [Manufacturing Manager—Hardwear]

Introduction

At the commencement of this research the main questions seemed to be (from chapter two):

- What is the character of IT diffusion and implementation in the companies?
- How is IT changing the general nature of managerial work?
- How are specific components of manager's work, namely communication, decision making and interpersonal matters being affected?
- To what extent are the implications of IT on managers dependent on existing management practices and cultures?

From these, and drawing on the literature, and on personal experience, the set of hypotheses in chapter three was formulated. This initial framework informed the field work which eventually ran to forty-nine visits to the five companies, and 101 interviews with managers. With the additional tool of the questionnaire survey, and taking into account the observation facilitated by such an extensive exposure to company environments, the revealed data are rich in detail. As the five companies were so different, not only in their organizational culture, structure and processes, but also in the extent, sophistication and pattern of IT, a very broad picture was obtained.

Using the systematic accumulation of managers' comments within the thirty-seven-element data base (described in chapter three) and with due regard to organizational function and hierarchical level of managers, the story for each company emerged. Integration of these stories into a coherent, though multi-faceted characterization was presented in chapter five. It remains for conclusions to be drawn and meanings to be wrought in this last chapter.

Results and the hypotheses

The hypotheses were a useful starting point. But as the field work proceeded, it became clear, even with a long personal experience of management in general, and the management of these companies in particular, that the nature of managerial work and its interaction with IT was much more interwoven than had been appreciated at the outset. The conclusions go significantly beyond the simple framework suggested by the hypotheses. Nevertheless, for completeness these hypotheses with brief comments derived from analysis of the data are set down here—a first approximation, as it were.

(1) The number of people reporting to any manager is decreasing.
Comment: The evidence is not unequivocal on this point. Certainly, the total number of staff in each company is reducing but so is the number of managers. Where IT is used extensively managers have smaller staff complements than hitherto.

(2) The proportion of professionals and skilled people in the subordinate group is increasing.
Comment: This was found in all companies.

(3) The responsibility of any manager for data and for artefacts is increasing.
Comment: The information management component of managers' work was everywhere gaining in importance. Also, managers are generally responsible for more technological hardware.

(4) The technical components (related to machines, data and systems) of any manager's role is increasing.
Comment: It is an important conclusion of this work that IT is increasing the 'technical' aspects of managers' roles, *vis-à-vis* 'social' components.

(5) Managers are increasingly using electronic data and message handling.
Comment: In Components 'e-mail' is used substantially; in the other four companies it is used hardly at all, though its use is growing slowly.

(6) Managerial activities concerned with integration and function boundary-crossing are increasing.
Comment: This was found in all companies.

(7) There is a diminution in the managers' greater access to data relative to permitted access of other role holders.
Comment: This was confirmed in general.

(8) The data progress-chasing activities of managers are decreasing.
Comment: Progress chasing seems so far not to be affected by IT.

(9) Planning is increasing and controlling is decreasing in the roles of managers.
Comment: Managers believed their time horizons were extended by IT and that they are giving more attention to 'formal' planning. On the other hand IT tends to weaken informal, personal planning due to its 'prompting' nature. The detailed 'monitoring of staff' component of managers' work seems to be decreasing.

(10) IT is producing local effects and concomitant effects distant from points of application.
Comment: This is a widespread feature and is called the 'field effect' of IT in this book.

(11) The IT system is carrying out increasingly higher 'intelligence' organizational processes previously carried out by people.
Comment: This was found in all companies.

(12) Organizational specificity in terms of data, timing and systems is increasing.
Comment: This was found in all the cases.

(13) The difference between management and non-management roles in terms of access is decreasing.
Comment: This was shown to be taking place widely.

(14) Management roles are becoming more team-like and less hierarchical.
Comment: This is taking place in all the companies in a general way but is most prominent where IT use is intensive.

(15) Organizational roles in general are becoming less routinized and call for more initiative-taking, and that management roles are becoming less definable in terms of routine.
Comment: This was commonly found to be happening.

(16) Managers' apparent activity rate is decreasing and reflective activities are increasing.
Comment: The very opposite of this was found everywhere. IT increases the pressure on managers to respond quickly; thus their 'pace' of work is increased and they have less time for reflection.

(17) As IT permeates an organization all roles gain more managerial activities, and the distinction between management and non-management roles decreases.

Comment: Intensive use of IT seems to blur distinctions between management and non-management roles and to increase management-type behaviour such as initiative-taking, flexibility and professionalism.

OVERALL CONCLUSIONS

The overall conclusions naturally go beyond the brief comments on the hypotheses set out above. Those conclusions, following the order throughout this thesis, are clustered into five groups, namely:

- Implementation
- The general character of managers' work
- People issues
- Communication
- Decision making

Implementation—Information technology consists of several interwoven technologies and processes entering organizations in:

- transaction processing—the systematized electronic processing of standardized elements of data handling;
- decision support for control, coordination and planning, at an organizational level, in any function and with any time horizon;
- electronic mail—messaging between people within the organization or between them and people in other organizations;
- networking—the provision of distributed terminals allowing rapid access to data banks and to computer analysis and synthesis. This may be communication between people and computers or between computers;
- control engineering associated with machine-accomplished physical processes.

IT developments are growing from precursors—telephones, telex, punched card machines and previous computers. There are no discontinuities, and in the short run, no revolution. However, the electronic technologies and their applications do possess distinct characteristics which are changing organizations and their management in radical directions in the longer run.

The unique culture of each organization is powerful in conditioning the exact IT diffusion, usage and implications. In all situations, there is some degree of contention between change-dominant techno-economic forces and change-resistant cultures, structures and practices. But this contention is neither simple, nor linear. Rather there is a multi-directional web of interests which is itself changing.

There has been an acceleration in recent years in managerial realization of the potential of IT and in the spread and use of the technology.

The reducing cost of hardware, especially of personal computers, is a strong influence in this.

With some exceptions, the most senior managers did not appear to be knowledgeable of or especially interested in the information technologies and were not leading the evolution of IT-based changes. Nor in any company was there an explicit strategy for IT in the sense of a laid-down and understood plan for introducing and using IT and for preparing people for new IT-based practices. Most managers believed IT diffusion and usage were matters of tactics.

The main dialectic to initiate decisions to install IT systems is between managers in the management information systems (MIS) function and directors. Accounting practice of cost/benefit analysis is widely regarded as acting against IT introduction due to the difficulties of quantifying benefits.

Practicabilities of implementation, usage and implications are worked out almost entirely at middle- and junior-management ranks. Most application initiatives come from MIS, though successful implementation depends greatly on key individuals—'champions'.

MIS staff had the overwhelming advantage of expert IT knowledge in discussions of applications with operating managers. However, user-managers generally regarded MIS staff as having inadequate understanding of management and organizational process, not least in the personnel dimension. Not surprisingly there was tension between system designers and users though this was not linear, rather it was convoluted by various levels of knowledge and enthusiasms among managers.

In no company was there close liaison between MIS and the personnel function, nor was IT and its implications given great consideration in organizational design.

In its earliest stages IT is applied at operational levels in the company. It then proceeds up the hierarchy converting increasingly complex and low-volume activities to computer-assisted operation. Early IT diffusion tends to follow a 'cost-reduction' imperative, but 'added value' later becomes important, though both these motivations operate together.

In no case was there a single responsibility for IT implementation. Instead, because IT applications involve several technologies (plant automation, office automation, telecommunications, software and so on), responsibilities are divided and often there was only weak coordination between the various applications of these technologies.

The general character of managers' work—The basic nature of managers' work is little changed by IT. It remains highly fragmented, weakly defined, action-orientated, with much attention-switching as managers continually re-assess their priorities. Oral communication continues to be a prominent feature.

Effects of IT on managers are various, depending specifically on the form and extent of the technology and the nature of each manager's practices and environment. In the short run the prevailing cultures strongly condition IT effects.

Although management has always been concerned with change, the current transitions being induced by IT are major and rapid. 'Management of change' will be a central focus for managers for the foreseeable future.

The balance of attention is changing for managers. IT is forcing a more technological orientation and causing managers to give more time and priority to information management.

As IT increases productivity and reduces numbers of people in organizations, the historical 'natural priority' of 'social managment' is being eroded. The amount of detailed personnel administration is reducing.

Because of the reduction in numbers of people, and the increase in professional skills of subordinates, the changing nature of information management and the weakening of 'designatory' structures, there is a greater tendency toward adaptive behaviour: termed 'the adaptive milieu' in this book. Smaller teams of staff with colleague-like relationships are beginning to replace the larger, more hierarchical functional groupings.

The classic tension between centralization and decentralization continues and is unresolved by IT. Some effects of IT, for instance increased organizational transparency, act toward centralization, while others like the increased pressure for subordinates to react quickly, force delegation, that is decentralization.

IT effects have so far mainly been on middle and junior managers: they are directly impacted by the issues of reducing staff, weakening of boundaries, more availability of data access and so on. However, senior managers are beginning to be affected by the encroachment of IT-driven decision support and the increasing awareness of the strategic influences of IT.

The greater organizational transparency, the rate of change and the new emphases on technical and systems matters are together increasing perceptions of vulnerability in managers.

Managers and people—IT is increasing productivity, and thus, for a given output, is reducing numbers of people. This 'higher productivity, smaller work force' tendency has a multitude of consequences for management.

Traditional, practical skills are disappearing; new conceptual skills related to information management and to operating in more creative, flexible, less routinized ways are developing. As these skills are required by both non-management staff (information workers) and managers (knowledge workers), to an extent differences between these roles are diminishing.

The priority of 'designatory' organizational structures is reducing: functions are more integrated, boundaries and tiers less defined. The previous rather 'skeletonized' and static nature of organizational structures is becoming more amorphous and dynamic. Patterns of interpersonal relationship and communication are thus less constrained. There is therefore a trend towards 'node-to-relevant-node' communication which may bypass some managers at times and increase uncertainty.

Management of people is becoming less dependent on hierarchical authority and more on leadership related to professional respect in a 'team culture'. This is due to a combination of a reducing workforce, more conceptual skills and increasing subordinate autonomy. This emerging 'adaptive milieu' places more focus on appropriateness to the task at hand and on development of responsiveness of individuals, practices and structures.

Managers and communication—Communication has always been for managers a composite of 'information management' and 'interpersonal communication', the latter being predominantly oral. It is the increasing effectiveness in information management which IT confers which creates the major consequences for managers.

Information management is becoming a more central component of managers' work. Use of terminals, and involvement in design, implementation and management of systems is expanding.

As the use of IT increases, data and systems redundancy reduces, as does the number of sub-systems. System tightness in terms of timing, format and synchronization between functionally based data procedures is increasing. Thus integration of activities is improving.

The reduction of specific data-ownership, the increased organizational transparency and the tendency toward 'node-to-relevant-node' communication increase uncertainty for managers.

Managers perceive an increase in paperwork with increasing IT and also increases in the amounts of data available. This creates problems of data relevancy and priority for managers.

Interpersonal communication, and that is mostly oral, remains at the heart of the management processes and is, as yet, little changed by IT.

Managers and decision making—At transactional processing levels, decisions are increasingly being absorbed into the computer system.

Because of reductions in numbers of staff, detailed personnel administration and associated decisions are reducing.

Computer decision-support is increasing though is mostly at operational and tactical levels.

Computer produced analyses and print-outs are widely used at all levels of management where IT is at a sophisticated stage of application.

Several effects of IT combine to produce greater uncertainty amongst managers which offsets the gains in information clarity, availability and speed of access conferred by IT.

Because IT tends to weaken certain aspects of conventional structures, it appears to be important for managers to have a strong consensus about company policy and strategy against which to take decisions.

Reflections

Although there has always been management, be it of religious orders, or sailing ships or armies, it is only in the last hundred years that it has become so thought about, written about and latterly, researched. A paradox runs through this century of examination: management is changing yet management is staying the same. Managing the sweat-shops and quill-pen offices of the nineteenth century must have been a world apart from the management of today's technologically based factories. And yet the essentially fragmentary, low-structured, action-orientation, oral nature of the manager's job remains. The application of IT in and around the work of managers in recent years does not seem to have changed this basic nature.

It would be tempting to conclude that the changes of history—from Satanic mill to electronic office—are then principally metamorphoses of *context*, leaving largely untouched the art and skills and practices of leadership and governance that management is. But this is not so. The historical unfolding of social, political, psychological, economic and technological factors, we may conclude, has always been conditioning management. Information technology is only one of current condition-ing factors and yet, for the reasons set out in this book, it has the potential for bringing large and radical change to management roles. For IT is transforming not only the organizational context, but also the balance, emphasis and practices of management work itself.

Although 'small is beautiful' has been with us since 1974, it is only since perhaps 1980 that the application of the electronic technologies, coupled with the current political and economic stringencies, has facili-tated a sea-change in the personnel dimension. Organizations are now on a downward trend in terms of size of labour force, a trend which I believe will continue.

All five companies in this study have had a history of a growing number of personnel until this decade. The two mechanical engineering companies, in particular, had organizational cultures, structures, practices—and problems—which resulted from a large and relatively unskilled population of workers. A complicated panoply of personnel

and industrial relations activities evolved. Strongly demarcated departments and hierarchy guided and inhibited managers. The continual
pressure of social management overwhelmed managers. While this
scenario was not universal in Britain, it is not untypical. Not surprisingly, the emphasis in management education and in manager development has been on social management. Theories of the social psychology
of management have been prolific, if not universally enlightening.

Now the numbers are declining, demarcations and dependence on
hierarchical authority are dissolving. The focus of managers is turning
from the many to the few. The social dynamics of this few, the team, will
be crucial, but it will be a different kind of management. Creativity,
initiative-taking, non-routine, fluid communications and attention to the
relevant and to the individual will be prime. And all this is already seen
at Components and in isolated cells elsewhere. In their important work
on innovation Burns and Stalker (1961) describe the 'organic' organization as being best suited to unstable conditions. I have built on this idea
in two ways. First, IT appears to be a destabilizing force pushing
organizations toward the more fluid, responsive culture, which is
termed here, 'the adaptive milieu'. Second, the effects of IT as set out in
this thesis go far beyond the mostly structural issues considered by
Burns and Stalker and include cultural and process adaptation. There
are echoes here also of the 'flexible specialization' discussed by Piore
and Sabel (1984).

This research shows also that the centre stage is being taken by
information management. Of course, taking sound decisions has always
been at the heart of effective management. And creating effective
information assembly, analysis and dissemination has always been
necessary for those sound decisions. Once again, 'plus ça change . . .'.
The difference is technology. Now, and in the future, managers have
available a systems technology of prodigious, and possibly unimagin-
able, power and speed. And from a management education and development viewpoint this is new. For although systems theory and
practice has been taught to computer specialists for decades, managers
are relatively naïve in this field. Not only that, but their natural propen-
sity is towards action, discussion, fragmented and reactive behaviour—
not towards reflective analysis and technological orientation.

Dynamic computer models of sections of the business, and eventually
the total business, updated in near-real time, with various formats and
elements instantly re-analysable and still a long way off. But it is in that
direction that management is moving. Much of the current tension and
confusion among managers is due to transition crises. They are being
called upon to encompass sophisticated technology and systems when
often their experience is of neither.

Unfortunately, as two recent reports (Handy, 1987, and Constable
and McCormick, 1987) show, management development in the United

Kingdom is extremely weak. This was basically the situation in the companies studied for this book: few interviewed managers had substantial management education either for management or for IT. The starting point for this research was my concern about the education, training and development of managers in relation to the ubiquitous and powerful new technologies. The research clearly shows that tomorrow's managers will need a much improved understanding (and skills to match) of team management, of technology and of systems. Probably technology has always been seminal for organizations, but with IT it is now inescapable that management is deeply implicated in technological issues.

There is then, and this is important, a need to integrate an understanding of technology and its effects into all management and business education and training, not least for the most senior managers. Such education and training would at least include:

(1) an appreciation of the several more-important technologies such as IT, biotechnology, opto-electronics, plastics and combination materials;
(2) an understanding of the historical development of technologies and their economic, social and political consequences;
(3) some focus on the contention between fast developing technologies and cultural-structural-social inertia, and solutions to these contention problems, and
(4) an extensive treatment of systems concepts and consequences for products and services, for organizational design and operations and for tasks and jobs.

But probably the main issue about management uncovered by this research is the corroboration of many reports over the last one hundred years: that education and training, and specifically that for managers, is woefully inadequate in the United Kingdom. We should not be at all surprised at the relatively unenthusiastic treatment of IT by many British managers, nor in the decline of the United Kingdom in economic terms over several decades, nor in the confusions and ineffectiveness frequently found in British organizations, private and public. The central problem must now be blindingly obvious: our whole society (for whatever reason) values education and training too little. And in particular there is a massive lack of well-educated and trained managers.

The managers in the studies described here were in general trying to do a sound job but were depending mostly on their native wit and common sense. Few had been given the professional preparation, the technical knowledge or the social-psychological skills that were needed to manage the highly complex technical and people issues.

And finally. In the long run IT will probably have wrought radical changes on business. In the shorter run the ongoing transitions are multi-dimensional and fiendishly difficult to understand. Organizations and their managers are, it seems, becoming more technological, systematized and adaptive. But to quote from the 1956 HMSO report on automation: 'Automation will not make robots of us all. On the contrary it will demand wider knowledge, greater ability and a higher degree of skill from worker and manager alike.'

Appendices

Appendix 1 Managers interviewed

Engineering

E.	Title (no. of interviews)	Function	Tier
1.	Financial director (1)	Finance	2
2.	Treasurer (1)	Finance	3
3.	Manager, computer systems (3)	Finance	3
4.	Manager, finance administration (2)	Finance	3
5.	Manager, systems and programming (2)	Finance	4
6.	Assistant treasurer (1)	Finance	4
7.	Manager, accounts payable (1)	Finance	5
8.	Manager, general accounting systems (1)	Finance	5
9.	Senior project leader (finance systems) (1)	Finance	5
10.	Senior user systems planner (1)	Finance	5
11.	Manager, provisions and payroll administration (1)	Finance	5
12.	Manager, organization and methods (1)	Finance	5
13.	Supply manager (1)	Supply	2
14.	Purchase manager (1)	Supply	3
15.	Manager, material scheduling and inventory control (1)	Supply	3
16.	Manager, cost control and statistics (1)	Supply	3
17.	Traffic staff manager (1)	Supply	3
18.	Manager, traffic planning and operation (1)	Supply	4
19.	Administrative assistant to marketing director (2)	Marketing	3
20.	Manager, marketing services (1)	Marketing	3
21.	Manager, field operations (1)	Marketing	3
22.	Manager, sales systems (1)	Marketing	4
23.	Manager, dealer communications systems (1)	Marketing	5
24.	Director, public affairs (1)	Public affairs	2

Engineering

25. Manager, reliability and quality control (1)	Quality control	2
26. Director of industrial relations (1)	Industrial relations	2
27. Personnel executive (3)	Personnel	3
28. Manager, management training (3)	Personnel	4
29. Training officer (1)	Personnel	5
30. Training officer (1)	Personnel	5

Hardwear

H. Title (no. of interviews)	Function	Tier
1. Managing director (3)		1
2. Information systems director (4)	Systems	2
3. Systems development manager (1)	Systems	3
4. Financial director (1)	Finance	2
5. Controller, manufacturing operations (2)	Finance	3
6. Liquidity controller (1)	Finance	3
7. Finance systems administration manager (1)	Finance	3
8. Technical director (4)	Technical	2
9. Manager, technical computing (1)	Technical	4
10. Director of manufacturing (3)	Manufacturing	2
11. Manager, manufacturing engineering (1)	Manufacturing	3
12. Manager, material flow (1)	Manufacturing	3
13. Manager, industrial engineering (1)	Manufacturing	4
14. Manager, manufacturing systems (2)	Manufacturing	4
15. Manager factory B (1)	Manufacturing	4
16. Manager factor C (1)	Manufacturing	4
17. Director of domestic marketing and sales (1)	Marketing	2
18. Manager, general sales (1)	Marketing	3
19. Manager, commercial systems (2)	Marketing	3
20. Manager, international distribution (1)	Marketing	3
21. Manager, domestic sales (1)	Marketing	4
22. Also several informal conversations with:		
training manager		3
manager, market communications		3

Fashion

F. Title (no. of interviews)	Function	Tier
1. Company chairman (1)	Finance	1
2. Director, finance and administration (1)	Finance	2
3. Production co-ordinator (3)	Manufacturing	3
4. General manager (2)	Manufacturing	3
5. Factory manager (2)	Manufacturing	4
6. General manager (1)	Marketing	3
7. Distribution manager (1)	Marketing	3
8. Senior merchandiser (1)	Marketing	4
9. Data processing manager A (1)	MIS	3

10. Data processing manager B (2)	MIS	4
11. Personnel director (4)	Personnel	2
Also several informal conversations with:		
managing director		2
and		
other factory managers		4

Integral

I. Title (no. of interviews)	Function	Tier
1. Managing director (1)	General	1
2. Divisional general manager (1)	General	2
3. Cost accountant (1)	Finance	4
4. Manager, computing services (1)	MIS	4
5. Engineering manager (1)	Technical	3
6. Manager, technical documentation (1)	Technical	4
7. Project leader (1)	Technical	5
8. Operations manager (1)	Manufacturing	3
9. Quality control manager (1)	Manufacturing	4
10. Manager, manufacturing (2)	Manufacturing	4
11. Product test manager (1)	Manufacturing	4
12. Production manager (2)	Manufacturing	5
13. Manager, production planning and control (1)	Manufacturing	5
14. Manager, strategic developments (1)	Marketing	2
15. Commercial manager (1)	Marketing	3
16. Company facilities manager (1)	Facilities	2
17. Personnel executive (1)	Personnel	2
18. Training officer (2)	Personnel	3
19. Site personnel officer (3)	Personnel	4

Components

C. Title (no. of interviews)	Function	Tier
1. General manager (1)	General	2
2. Corporate entity controller (1)	Finance	3
3. Branch manager (1)	Technical	2
4. Product engineering manager (1)	Technical	4
5. Manager, manufacturing A (1)	Manufacturing	3
6. Manager, manufacturing B (1)	Manufacturing	3
7. Planning manager (1)	Manufacturing	3
8. UK marketing manager (1)	Marketing	3
9. European marketing manager (1)	Marketing	3
10. Product marketing manager A (1)	Marketing	3
11. Marketing operations manager (1)	Marketing	4
12. Product test manager (1)	Marketing	4
13. Production manager (2)	Marketing	5

Components

14. Manager, production planning (1)	MIS	4
15. Personnel director (3)	Personnel	2
16. Personnel manager A (1)	Personnel	3
17. Personnel manager B (1)	Personnel	3
18. UK facilities manager (1)	Facilities	3

Also several informal conversations with
    personal assistant to personnel director

Appendix 2 Interview formats

RESEARCH
14.10.84
JMJ/MPMS

(Format 1 was used in discussions with other researchers)

INTERVIEW FORMAT 2
(Used for pilot interviews)

COMPANY _____ Analysis Sheet Completed

INTERVIEW REF _____ _____

1. Name of Manager   Age _____

2. Title

3. Internal Phone   Office Location

4. Qualifications

5. Experience

6. Current Responsibilities

7. Skills/knowledge re IT—What IT courses have you attended?

8. What knowledge/skills on IT do you have? (Beyond awareness)

9. What do you feel about IT?

10. How would you characterize IT in this company?

11. Who are the key people in this company for IT?

12. Which departments are developing IT fastest?

13. What IT applications are you currently involved with?

14. How is IT strategy determined?

15. Why are these applications taking place?

16. Where does push to use these applications come from:
    Management above?
    Interviewee?
    Staff below?
    DP staff?
    Other managers?

17. Are applications analysed post event?

18. What % of your own role is now somehow IT/systems related? Explain.

19. What other management roles have reduced?

20. How do you expect IT/systems to develop in or around you role?

21. Is you role changing because of IT? How and why?

    Checklist
    IT knowledge
    Emphasis on:
       people
       data
       technical equipment
    Authority
    Responsibility
    Clarity of role
    Initiative-taking
    Boundary-crossing
    Time span of discretion

22. Are you altering the structure or processes within your sphere of responsibility because of IT? How and why? Be specific.

    Checklist
    Section organization
    Number of managers/supervisors
    Number of professionals
    Total number of staff
    Vertical tiers
    Delegation
    Decision making
    People reporting to you directly
    Communication (within section)
    Clarity of tasks—specialization
    Training

23. How are the structures/processes changing between your section and the rest of the company as a result of IT?

    Checklist
    Functional demarcation
    Data flows
    Decisions
    Communication
    Clarity of tasks
    Flexibility/rigidity
    Ownership of data
    Top management interventions

24. How is IT changing the knowledge/skills you require to be effective?

25. Is IT systems being developed too slowly/too fast in your section? Why is this? What are you doing about this?

INTERVIEW FORMAT 3   RESEARCH
(Used for 95 per cent of interviews)   17.01.85
JMJ/MPMS

In data base

COMPANY _____ INTERVIEW REF _____

1. Name of manager   Age _____

2. Title

3. Internal phone

4. Office location

5. Qualifications

6. Experience

7. Current responsibilities

8. Tier number (MD = 1)

9. Number of people reporting to you directly

10. Classification of subordinates and changes in the last 5 years:

    Managers
    Professionals
    Skilled clerical
    Unskilled clerical
    Skilled manual
    Unskilled manual

11. How does IT affect your job?

    Prompts:
      Micros
      Systems
      Data

12. Why is IT being used more in your area?

13. Which people do you communicate with? How? How often? On what issues? Is IT changing this in any way?

    Prompt:
      VDU/Terminal

14. How do you use your time? Is this changing due to IT?

    Prompts:
      Routines in role
      Flexibility
      Initiative taking
      Activity pace
      Decisions

15. What people issues do you get involved with? Any changes related to IT?

    Prompts:
    Relations with staff
    Collegiate vs hierarchy

16. What systems or data issues do you get involved with? Any changes because of IT?

    Prompts:
    Timeliness of data
    Clarity of data
    Access to data—self
    Access to data—subordinates
    Amounts of data
    Control of data
    Systems design
    Systems improvement
    Systems links with other departments
    Systems links outside company

17. What other departments do you most relate to? How? Why? Is this changing because of IT?

18. What planning do you do?

    Prompts:
    Time for reflection
    Time horizons
    Strategy

19. How are you preparing for the future?

    Prompts:
    Current knowledge of IT
    Own training
    Staff training

Appendix 3 Compilation of questionnaires

For each question (5 to 38) managers were asked to compare their present job situation to that pertaining five years previously and to tick a five-tone scale:

Increased			*Decreased*	
20%	10%	Stayed the same	10%	20%
1	2	3	4	5

In the subsequent analysis these tones were rated 9, 7, 5, 3 and 1 respectively for 1, 2, 3, 4 and 5.

Thus the following figures show approximately the degree of increase (above 50), or decrease (below 50) in each subject as perceived by managers. For instance the answers to question 9 (clustering around 70) suggest a perception of considerably increased quantities of information.

Notes:

1. B/C = 'IT-involved' managers.
   D   = 'less IT-involved' managers.
2. Specialist IT managers are excluded from both groups. Thus overall rating is not necessarily the mean of B/C and D ratings.
3. At Components it was not possible to discriminate between B/C and D managers.
4. The full questionnaire formats are in Appendix 4.

NOTE: The figures show approximately the degree of increase (above 50), or decrease (below 50) in each subject as perceived by managers.

A *Information Issues*

	All Managers	Engineering			Hardwear			Fashion			Integral			Components
		Overall	B/C	D	Overall	B/C	D	Overall	B/C	D	Overall	B/C	D	Overall (B/C & D not separated)
5. My time chasing information has	59	53	43	44	56	52	58	63	66	70	52	43	59	66
6. Paperwork in my job has	63	58	45	52	57	60	53	70	58	80	56	66	47	73
7. My involvement with information gathering, analysis and dissemination has	70	70	70	65	67	75	60	73	55	83	73	62	70	69
8. The usefulness of printed information available to me has	65	66	64	65	73	70	59	70	82	60	62	60	61	66
9. The quantity of information which I use in my job has	77	75	73	73	74	78	66	77	82	70	72	80	61	81
10. The access of *my* immediate subordinates to information available to *me* has	70	72	73	73	72	72	63	70	80	63	62	60	63	73
11. The difficulties in understanding the information I get have	49	45	48	46	50	47	52	45	38	57	52	53	36	53

12. The 'timeliness' (= arriving in time to be useful) of information available to me has	61	62	58	59	61	68	52	63	74	60	53	63	44	65
B *Subordinates*														
13. Number of subordinates reporting *to* most of *my* 1st line supervisors has	48	44	38	50	43	43	50	46	50	40	42	36	50	63
14. The number of professionals and skilled people amongst *my* subordinates has	55	57	58	53	47	46	61	41	50	30	35	27	46	73
15. The 'management of people' content of *my immediate subordinates has*	59	65	48	60	47	43	56	59	70	50	51	50	56	64
16. Time spent talking with my immediate subordinates has	66	65	70	60	66	72	64	63	65	66	62	67	63	66
17. *My* time on 'people' issues has	69	68	73	65	73	75	77	65	65	73	64	67	61	69
18. The problems of getting skilled staff has	68	55	53	58	72	70	53	72	70	83	68	73	64	68

NOTE: The figures show approximately the degree of increase (above 50), or decrease (below 50) in each subject as perceived by managers.

	All Managers	Engineering			Hardwear			Fashion			Integral			Components
		Overall	B/C	D	Overall	B/C	D	Overall	B/C	D	Overall	B/C	D	Overall (B/C & D not separated)
C *Information Technology*														
19. My involvement with systems/computers has	77	75	83	66	75	83	68	73	86	52	75	80	70	81
20. My knowledge of computers/systems has	82	75	78	68	73	82	66	80	86	73	81	73	76	78
21. My use of electronic data bases has	76	78	85	66	68	82	52	72	86	56	73	87	74	85
D *Your Role*														
22. My involvement in industrial relations issues has	59	57	68	56	58	57	54	61	70	63	62	63	61	62
23. My authority to take decisions has	65	66	70	59	61	68	52	67	50	80	56	37	73	71
24. The complexities in taking decisions has	66	59	54	57	63	70	52	64	40	77	65	53	76	77

25. My emphasis on strategy (as distinct from short term tactics) has	68	65	68	63	64	72	45	72	60	73	65	53	76	71
26. My amount of consultation with managers senior to me, has	62	59	65	52	62	62	53	67	70	63	55	43	64	63
27. The formality in my role has	53	42	40	50	49	52	46	68	70	67	47	46	47	57
E. *Use Of Your Time*														
28. Time spent dealing with other departments in my company has	63	65	73	59	60	64	57	72	74	70	53	47	59	66
29. My time spent on *routine* activities has	47	45	42	53	43	43	52	58	46	67	35	40	41	49
30. My time for reflection has	43	41	46	39	42	48	43	60	66	53	52	57	47	37
31. The pace of my job has	72	75	69	68	69	77	66	65	46	80	67	66	67	77
32. The time ahead (in weeks) and I focus on mainly has	61	59	48	66	59	65	47	63	66	63	64	60	67	66
F. *Organization Matters*														
33. The organizational influence of the company's computer department has	64	58	53	61	71	70	70	78	82	73	64	73	56	57

NOTE: The figures show approximately the degree of increase (above 50), or decrease (below 50) in each subject as perceived by managers.

	All Managers	Engineering			Hardwear			Fashion			Integral			Components
		Overall	B/C	D	Overall	B/C	D	Overall	B/C	D	Overall	B/C	D	Overall (B/C & D not separated)
34. The number of tiers of management in my company has	50	38	35	34	46	46	49	48	50	46	67	80	56	55
35. The difficulties in knowing who I should communicate with (in the company) have	48	47	50	48	40	44	43	55	42	57	48	63	36	49
36. The understanding of my senior managers, of work done in my section, has	55	57	58	59	48	52	43	62	70	53	55	60	50	59
37. The number of rules and regulations in my job has	59	55	60	50	57	55	63	58	54	63	65	70	61	60
38. The 'planning' elements in my role have	69	67	70	63	76	72	52	72	70	77	66	67	79	71

Appendix 4 Questionnaires

JMJ/MS   23.05.85

Questionnaire 'A'

Thank you for helping with this research. It is trying to discover how managers' roles are changing.

'IT' = information technology = computers + systems + telecommunications + automation.

Company ....

1. (a) Your name (capitals) .... Your Age ....

   (c) Title .... Years in this post ....

   (d) Your qualifications (academic and professional) ....

   ....

   ....

   (e) Your current responsibilities very briefly ....

   ....

   (f) Your tier number now (Managing Director = 1) ....
       (Managers reporting to MD tier = 2)

   (g) Your tier number in 1980 ....

2. Number of people reporting to you now *directly* ....

3. Total number of people for whom you are responsible ....

4. Classification of people for whom you are responsible and changings in numbers of *these* people in the last 5 years, i.e. compare your present section/ department with the same section/department 5 years ago.

	Number Now	Approx No in 1980
Managers or Supervisors eg Warehouse Manager, Sales Administrative Supervisor		
Professionals eg Qualified Accountants, Qualified Engineers (without manage- ment responsibility)		
Skilled Clerical (probably not professionally qualified)		
Unskilled Clerical eg filing clerk		
Skilled manual		
Unskilled Manual		

Please tick appropriate box. Comments refer to your own job in your own organisation. *Compare the present with 5 years ago.*	1 20% Increased	2 10% Increased	3 Stayed the same	4 10% Decreased	5 20% Decreased
A *Information Issues*					
5. My time chasing information has					
6. Paperwork in my job has					
7. My involvement with information gathering, analysis and dissemination has					
8. The usefulness of printed information available to me has					
9. The quantity of information which I use in my job has					
10. The access of *my* immediate subordinates to information available to *me* has					
11. The difficulties in understanding the information I get have					
12. The "timeliness" (= arriving in time to be useful) of information available to me has					
B *Subordinates (to my present function)*					
13. Number of subordinates reporting *to* most of *my* 1st line supervisors has					
14. The number of professionals and skilled people amongst *my* subordinates has					
15. The "management of people" content of *my immediate subordinates* has					

Please tick appropriate box. Comments refer to your own job in your own organisation. *Compare the present with 5 years ago.* B *Subordinates (to my present function)* (continued)	1 20% Increased	2 10% Increased	3 Stayed the same	4 10% Decreased	5 20% Decreased
16. Time spent talking with my immediate subordinates has					
17. *My* time on "people" issues has					
18. The problems of getting skilled staff has					
C *Information Technology*					
19. My involvement with systems/ computers has					
20. My knowledge of computers/ systems has					
21. My use of electronic data bases has					
D *Your Role*					
22. My involvement in industrial relations issues has					
23. My authority to take decisions has					
24. The complexities in taking decisions has					
25. My emphasis on strategy (as distinct from short term tactics) has					
26. My amount of consultation with managers senior to me, has					
27. The formality in my role has					

Please tick appropriate box. Comments refer to your own job in your own organisation. *Compare the present with 5 years ago.*	1 20% Increased	2 10% Increased	3 Stayed the same	4 10% Decreased	5 20% Decreased
E *Use of your time*					
28. Time spent dealing with other departments in my company has					
29. My time spent on *routine* activities has					
30. My time for reflection has					
31. The pace of my job has					
32. The time ahead (in weeks) that I focus on mainly has					
F *Organisation Matters*					
33. The organisational influence of the company's computer department has					
34. The number of tiers of management in my company has					
35. The difficulties in knowing who I should communicate with (in my company) have					
36. The understanding of my senior managers, of work done in my section, has					
37. The number of rules and regulations in my job has					
38. The "planning" elements in my role have					

RESEARCH
23.05.85
JMJ/MS

Questionnaire 'B'—Company data

The purpose of this questionnaire is to establish the size of your company, and any changes in size, and to give an idea of your products.

Thank you for helping in this survey.

1. Company name ....

2. If the company is part of a group would you briefly explain:

   ....

   ....

   ....

3. Total UK employees ....

4. Total employees in this location (approx)

1985	1982	1980
....	....	....

5. Total number of managers (excluding supervisors) at this location:

   .... in 1985

   .... in 1980

6. Total number of supervisors (in addition to managers) at this location:

   .... in 1985

   .... in 1980

7. Total sales revenue from this site

1984	1982	1980
....	....	....

8. Product range:

Questionnaire 'C'—Information technology

IT = computers + systems; automation; telecommunications

The purpose of this questionnaire is to establish the factual history of the development and use of information technology in your company. Looking back over that history, can you identify different 'periods' in the use of computers (etc)—for instance based on different hardware, or on adopting new systems. Assuming you can divide these developments into a number of 'periods' would you fill in one of these forms for *each period*.

1. Company ....

2. Brief description of the period:

   ....

   ....

   ....

3. Approximate dates of that period ....

4. Main computer/s (types) at that time ....

5. Principal applications of the computer at that time:

   ....

   ....

   ....

6. Number of people in data processing operations in that period ....

7. Operations mode of your computer during period:

   % batch entry   ......

   % remote job entry ......

   % on-line   ......

8. Numbers of (at this location only):

   8.1 Personal computers/micros   ......

   8.2 Terminals other than main computer   ......

   8.3 Mini computers other than main computer ......

   8.4 Management work stations   ......

   8.5 Word processing stations   ......

   8.6 CAD displays   ......

   8.7 CNC machines on shop floors   ......

   8.8 Robots   ......

   8.9 Other   ......

9. If you would like to add your own comments about this period, that would be helpful:

References

Aaron, J.D. (1969), 'Information systems in perspective', *Computing Surveys*, 1, No. 4, 213–16.

Abernathy, W.J. and Townsend, P.L. (1975), *Technological Forecasting and Social Change*, July.

Adair, J. (1968), *Training for Leadership*, Macdonald.

Alderson, W. (1965), *Dynamic Marketing Behaviour*, Homewood, Illinois.

Allen, B. (1982), 'An unmanaged computer system can stop you dead', *Harvard Business Review*, Nov.–Dec., 77–87.

Alvey, Programme (1985), *Annual Report*, IEE Publishing, Stevenage, November.

American Assembly of Collegiate Schools of Business, and the European Foundation for Management Development, 'The changing expectations of society in the next thirty years', Windsor Castle Colloquium, February 1979.

Ansoff, H. Igor (1965), *Corporate Strategy*, Penguin.

Anthony, P. (1986), *The Foundation of Management*, Tavistock, London.

Anthony, R.N. (1965), *Planning and Control Systems: A Framework for Analysis*, Harvard Graduate School of Business Administration, Boston.

Argyle, M. (1967). *The Psychology of Interpersonal Behaviour*, Pelican.

Argyris, C. (1977), *Double-loop learning in organizations*, Harvard Business Review, No. 55, 115–25.

Armstrong, Philip (1984), *Technical Change and Reductions in Life Hours of Work*, Technical Change Centre, April.

Baker, Kenneth, MP (1980), 'Information technology industrial and employment opportunities', *The Royal Society of Arts Journal*, **CXXX**, No. 5316, 780–90.

Bannon, L., Barr, J. and Holst, O. (eds) (1982), *Information Technology: Impact on the Way of Life*, Tycooly International Publishing, Dublin.

Barnard, C.I. (1938), *The Functions of the Executive*, Harvard University Press, Cambridge, Mass.

Barnet, Corelli (1986), *Audit of War*, Macmillan, London.

— (1974), *Strategy and Society*, Manchester University Press, Manchester.

Barras, R. and Swann, J. (1983), *The Adoption and Impact of Information Technology in the U.K. Insurance Industry*, Technological Change Centre, London.

Barron, I. and Curnow, R. (1979), *The Future with Microelectronics*, Frances Pinter, London.

Bartlett, F. (1958), *Thinking: An Experimental and Social Study*, Allen and Unwin, London.

Beck, William S. (1959), *Modern Science and the Nature of Life*, Harcourt Brace, New York.

Beer, S. (1975), *Platform for Change*, Wiley.

— (1972), *Brain of the Firm: The Managerial Cybernetics of Organisation*, The Penguin Press, London.

— (1959), *Cybernetics and Management*, English Universities Press, London.

Bell, C. and Newby, H. (eds) (1977), *Doing Sociological Research*, Allen and Unwin, London.

— and Roberts, H. (1984), *Social Researching—Politics, Problems, Practice*, Routledge Kegan Paul.

Bell, D. (1973), *The Coming of Post-Industrial Society*, Basic Books, New York.

Bell, R.M. (1983), *The Behaviour of Labour, Technical Change and the Competitive Weakness of British Manufacturing*, Technical Change Centre, London.

Bessant, J. (1983), 'Management and manufacturing innovation: the case of I.T.' in G. Winch (ed.), *Information Technology in Manufacturing Processes: Case Studies in Technological Change*, Rossendale, London.

— (1981), *The Impact of Microelectronics. Report and Bibliography*, Frances Pinter, London.

— (1980), *Factors Influencing Introduction of New Manufacturing Technology*, Technology Policy Unit, Aston University.

— (1979), 'Preparing for design studies. Ways of watching', *Design Studies*, **1**, No. 2.

—, Bowen, A., Dickson, K. and Marsh, J. (1981), *The Impact of Micro-electronics*, Frances Pinter, London.

Bessant, J. and Dickson, K. (1982a), *Issues in the Adoption of Micro-electronics*, Frances Pinter, London.

Bessant, J. and Dickson, K.E. (1982b), *Computers and Employment: A Selected Bibliography*, Heyden and Son, British Computer Society. London.

— and Grunt, M. (1985), *Management and Manufacturing Innovation in United Kingdom and West Germany*, Gower, Aldershot.

— and Haywood, B. (1986), *Flexibility in Manufacturing Systems. Omega. International Journal of Management Science*, **14**, No. 6, 465–73.

—, Lamming, R. and Arnold E. (1984), *Human Factors in Systems Design for Computer-Integrated Manufacturing*, Proceedings of 1st International Conference on Human Factors in Manufacturing, London, April.

Boddy, B. and Buchanan, D.A. (1982), 'Information technology and the experience of work' in L. Bannon, U. Barry and O. Holst (eds), *Information Technology Impact on the Way of Life*, Tycooly, Dublin.

Bohr, N. (1934), *Atomic Theory and Description of Nature*, Cambridge University Press, Cambridge.

Braverman, H. (1978), *Labour and Monopoly Capital: the Degradation of Work in the 20th Century*, Monthly Review Press, New York.

Brech, E.F.L. (ed.) (1953), *The Principles and Practice of Management*, Longmans, London.

Bright, J.R. (1958), *Automation and Management*, Harvard Business School, Division of Research, Boston.

Buchanan, D.A. (1982), 'Using the new technology: management objectives and organizational choices, *European Journal of Management*, **1**, No. 2, 70–9.

— and Boddy, D. (1983), *Organizations in the Computer Age; Technological Imperatives and Strategic Choice*, Gower, Aldershot.

— and Boddy, D. (1982), 'Advanced technology and the quality of working life: the effects of word processing on video typists', *Journal of Occupational Psychology*, **55**, 1–11.

Burns, Alan (1984), *New Information Technology*, Ellis Horwood, Chichester.

—, Newby, M. and Winterton, J. (undated), *Technology and the Restructuring of Work in British Coal Mining*, Working Environment Research Group, University of Bradford, (Mimeo).

Burns, T. (1957), 'Management in action', *Operational Research Quarterly*, **8**, 45–60.

— and Stalker, G.M. (1961), *The Management of Innovation*, Tavistock.

Butler Cox Report (1986), *Information Technology: Value for Money*, Butler Cox, London.

Campbell, J.P., Dunnette, M.D., Lawler, E.E., and Weick, K.E. (1970), *Managerial Behavior, Performance and Effectiveness*, McGraw-Hill, New York.

Cannon, T. (1984), *Customer Orientated Technological Futures for Library Systems*, August, (Mimeo).

Capra, F. (1975), *The Tao of Physics*, Fontana.

Carlson, S. (1951), *Executive Behaviour*, Stranberg, Stockholm.

Cherry, C. (1957), *On Human Communication*, MIT Press, Cambridge, Mass.

Child, J. (1984), 'New technology and developments in management organisation', *Omega*, **12**, No. 3.

— (1977), *Organization*, Harper and Row, London.

— and Y. Keiser A. (1977), 'The development of organizations over time in W.H. Starbuck (ed.), *Handbook of Organizational Design*, vol. 1, Elsevier.

— and Mansfield, R. (1972), 'Technology, size and organization structure', *Sociology*, **6**, 369–93.

Churchill, N.C., Kempster, J.H. and Uretsky, M. (1969), *Computer-based Information Systems for Management: A Survey*, National Association of Accountants, New York.

Clarke, J., Jacobs, A., King, R. and Rose, H. (1984), 'Industrial relations, new technology and divisions within the workforce, *Industrial Relations Journal*.

Collins, A.C. (1983), 'A management strategy for information processing: 1—the Segas case, *Long Range Planning*, **16**, No. 5, 29–44.

— (1984), 'A management strategy for information processing: 3—management information requirements', *Long Range Planning*, **17**, No. 1, 33–42.

Constable, C.J. (1971), *A Note on the Evaluation of Computer Process Control Systems*, Case Clearing House of Gt. Britain and Ireland, Cranfield Institute of Technology, Bedford.

Constable, J. and McCormick, R. (1987), *The Making of British Managers*, BIM and CBI Report, April, London.

Cooley, M.J.E. (1980), *Architect or Bee*, Langley Technical Service, Slough.

Coverdale, R. (1968), *Thought—A Frame for Teamwork*, Coverdale Training Ltd.

Cowling, A. and Evans, A. (1985), 'Organization planning and the role of the personnel department', *Personnel Review*, **14**, 9–15.

Cressey, P. and McInnes, J. (1980), 'Voting for Ford: industrial democracy and the control of labour', *Capital and Class*, **11**.

Crompton, R. and Reid, S. (1983), 'The deskilling of clerical work' in S. Wood (ed.), *The Degradation of Work*, Hutchinson, London.

Cunningham, W. (1903), *The Growth of English Industrial History and Commerce in Modern Times*, Cambridge University Press, Cambridge.

Cyert, R.M. and March, J.G. (1963), *A Behavioral Theory of the Firm*, Prentice-Hall, New York.

Daft, R.L. and Macintosh, N.B. (1981), 'A tentative exploration into the amount and equivocality of information processing in organisational work units', *Administrative Science Quarterly*, **26**, 207–24.

Dalton, M. (1959), *Men Who Manage*, Wiley, New York.

Dalton, G.W., Lawrence, P.R. and Lorsch, J.W. (eds) (1970), *Organizational Structure and Design*, Irvine-Dorsey.

Daniel, T.L. (1985), 'Managerial behaviour: their relationship to perceived organizational climate in a high-technology company', *Group Organization Studies*, **10**, No. 4, 1985.

Danzin, A. (1983), in H.J. Otway and M. Peltu (eds), *The Nature of New Office Technology*, Frances Pinter, London.

Davies, J. and Easterby-Smith, M. (1985), 'Organizational myths from the perspective of evaluation', paper presented at Association of Teachers of Management Conference, Ashridge, January.

Davis, Gordon B. (1974), *Management Information Systems: Conceptual Foundations, Structures and Development*, McGraw-Hill.

Dawson, P. and McLoughlin, I. (1984), 'Computer technology and the redefinition of supervision: a study of the effects of computerisation on railway freight supervisors, paper for British Sociological Association, April.

Deal, T.E. and Kennedy, A. (1982), *Corporate Cultures: The Rites and Rituals of Corporate Life*, Addison Wesley.

Dearden, J. (1983), 'Will the computer change the job of top management?', *Sloan Management Review*, Fall.

Delaney, W. (1960), 'Some field notes on the problems of access in organisation research, *Administrative Science Quarterly*, 448–57.

Denzin, N. (1970), *The Research Act in Sociology*, Aldine, Chicago.

Department of Scientific and Industrial Research (1956), *Automation: A Report on the Technical Trends and their Impact on Management and Labour*, HMSO.

Dewar, R. and Hage, J. (1978), 'Size, technology, complexity and structural differentiation towards a theoretical synthesis', *Administrative Science Quarterly*, **23**, 111–36.

Doubleday, C.F., Probert, D.E. and Walsham, G. (1983), 'A strategic model of communication demand', *Omega*, **11**, No. 4, 343–54.

Doswell, A. (1983), *Office Automation*, John Wiley and Sons, London.

Drucker, Peter F. (1982), *The Changing World of the Executive*, Heinemann.

Drury, D.H. (1983), 'An empirical assessment of the stages of D.P. growth', *Management Information Systems Quarterly*, June, 59–71.

Dubin, R. and Spray, S.L. (1964), 'Executive behaviour and interaction', *Industrial Relations*, **3**, 99–108.

Dummer, G.W.A. (1977), *Electronic Inventions, 1745–1976*, Pergamon Press, Oxford.

Eason, K.D. (1982), 'The process of introducing information technology', *Behaviour and Information Technology*, **1**, No. 2, April–June.

Egelholf, W.G. (1982), 'Strategy and structure in multi-national corporations: an information processing approach', *Administrative Science Quarterly*, **27**, 435–58.

Electronics and Power, Special Issue (1985), January.

Engwall, L. (1982), 'Organization theory: where are you?', *Omega*, **10**, No. 2, 125–34.

Ennals, R. and Cotterell, A. (1985), *Fifth Generation Computers—Their Implications for Further Education*, Further Education Unit, Department of Education and Science, London.

EOSYS Report (1986), *Top Executives and Information Technology: Disappointed Expectations*, EOSYS.

Evans, C. (1979), *The Mighty Micro*, Gollancz.

Eysenck, H.J. (1965), *Fact and Fiction in Psychology*, Penguin.

FAST (1984), *Objectives and Work Programme*, Commission of the European Committee, Brussels, February.

Fayol, H. (1916), *Administration Industrielle and Generale—Prevoyance, Organisation, Commandement, Co-ordination, Controle*, Bulletin de la Societe de L'industrielle Minerale.

Feigenbaum, E.A. (1980), *Expert Systems in the 1980's*, Proceedings: State of the Art Review 1980, Infotech, Maidenhead.

Fiedler, F. (1967), *A Theory of Leadership Effectiveness*, McGraw-Hill, New York.

Franko, L.G. (1976), *The European Multinationals*, Harper and Row.

Friedman, A.L. (1983), *Managerial, Organizational and Industrial Relations Implications of Advances in Data Processing and Information Technology: Survey of Research*, SSRC report HG 1314/11, March.

Friedman, L. (1985), *Managerial Strategies, Activities, Techniques and Technology: Towards a Complex Theory of the Labour Process* (Mimeo), March.

Friedrichs, G. and Schaff, A. (eds) (1982), *Microelectronics and Society: For Better or for Worse. A report to the Club of Rome*, Pergamon Press.

Galbraith, J.R. (1977), *Organizational Design*, Addison-Wesley.

— (1973), *Designing Complex Organizations*, Addison-Wesley.

Gantt, H.L. (1919), *Organising for Work*, Harcourt, Brace and Hove.

Gassmann, H.P. (ed) (1981), *Information, Computer and Communications Policies for the 1980's. An OECD report*, North-Holland, Amsterdam.

Gershuny, J. and Miles, I. (1983), *The New Service Economy*, Frances Pinter, London.

Gerwin, D. (1979), 'Relationships between structure and technology at the organisational and job levels', *Journal of Management Studies*, **16**, No. 1, 70–9.

— and Tarondeau, J.C. (1981), *Uncertainty and the Innovation Process for Computer Integrated Manufacturing Systems: Four Case Studies*, School of Business Administration Working Paper, University of Wisconsin, Milwaukee.

Gibson, C.F. and Nolan, R.L. (1974), 'Managing the four stages of E.D.P. growth', *Harvard Business Review*, January–February, 76–89.

Gilbreth, F.B. (1920), *Applied Motion Study*, Macmillan.

Gleave, David, (0000), *The Relationship between Labour and Mobility and Technical Change*, Technical Change Centre, London.

Godet, M. (1986), 'From the technological mirage to the social breakthrough', *Futures*, **18**, No. 3.

Gold, B. (1980), 'On the adoption of technological decision making in industry—superficial models and complex decision processes, *Omega*, **8**, No. 5.

Gorry, G.A. and Scott Morton, M.S. (1971), 'A framework for management information systems', *Sloan Management Review*, **13**, No. 1, 55–70.

Gouldner, A. (1967), *Enter Plato*, Routledge and Kegan Paul, London.

Green, K., Coombs, R. and Holroyd, K. (1980), *The Effects of Microelectronics Technologies on Employment Prospects. A Case Study of Tameside*, Gower, Aldershot.

Hage, J., Aitken, M. and Marrett, C.B. (1971), 'Organization structure and communications', *American Sociological Review*, **36**, 860–71.

Handy, C. (1987), *Managers in Five Countries: A New Professionalism*, NEDO and MSC Report, April.

— (1976), *Understanding Organizations*, Penguin, London.

Hartmann, G., Nicholas, I., Sorge, A. and Warner, M. (1983), 'Computerized machine tools, manpower consequences and skill utilization: a study of British and West German manufacturing firms', *British Journal of Industrial Relations*, **XXI**, No. 2.

Hay, A.C. and Majluf, N.S. (1981), 'Organizational design: a survey and an approach', *Operations Research*, **29**, No. 3, 417–47.

Head, R.V. (1967), 'Management information systems: a critical appraisal', *Datamation*, May, 23.

Hedberg, B. (1980), 'The design and impact of real-time computer systems: a case study of a Swedish commercial bank', in N. Bjorn-Anderson, B. Hedberg, D. Mercer, E. Mumford and A. Sole (eds), *The Impact of System Change in Organisations*, Sijtoff and Noordhoff, Alphen, Aan Den Rijn.

Heller, F. (1971), *Managerial Decision Making: A Study of Leadership Styles and Power Sharing*, Tavistock, London.

Hemphill, J.K. (1960), *Dimensions of Executive Positions: Research Monograph*, Ohio State University.

Herzberg, F. (1966), *Work and the Nature of Man*, World Publishing, Cleveland.

Hickson, D.J. *et al.* (1969), 'Operations technology and organization structure: an empirical appraisal', *Administrative Science Quarterly*, **14**, No. 3, 379–97, 1969.

Hirshheim, R. (1983), *Participative Systems Design: Some Conclusions from an Exploratory Study*, London School of Economics Working Paper, December, London.

Hobsbawn, E. (1968), *Industry and Empire*, Pelican.

Hodges, H.A. (1944), *Wilhelm Dilthey: An Introduction*, London.

Hodgson, R. *et al.* (1965), *The Executive Role Constellation: An Analysis of Personality and Role Relations in Management*, Harvard Business School Research Division, Boston.

Hofer, C.W. and Schendel, D. (1978), *Strategy Formulation: Analytical Concepts*, West, St Paul.

Homans, S. (1949), *The Human Group*, Wiley.

Huber, G. (1982), 'Organizational information systems: determinants of their performance and behaviour', *Management Science*, **28**, No. 2, 138–55.

Hurrion, R.M. (1976), 'The design, use and required facilities of an interactive visual computer simulation language to explore production planning, Ph.D. thesis, University of London.

Ilan, Y. and Shapira, Z. (1986), 'The introduction and use of microcomputers by professionals in an industrial corporation', *Technological Forecasting and Social Change*, **29**, 183–94.

Institute of Administrative Management and DTI (1984), *The Barriers and the Opportunities of I.T.—A Management Perspective*, Kearney, Management Consultants.

Irvine, J. and Martin, B.R. (1984), *Foresight in Science: Picking the Winners*, Frances Pinter, London.

Jenkins, C. and Sherman, B. (1979), *The Collapse of Work*, Eyre Methuen, London.

Jones, Daniel T. (1983), 'Technology and the UK Automobile Industry', *Lloyds Bank Review*, April, 14–25.

Kaplan, R.S. (1986a) 'Must C.I.M. be justified by faith alone?', *Harvard Business Review*, No. 2.

Kaplan, R.S. (1986b), *Accounting Log: The Obsolescence of Cost Accounting Systems in the Uneasy Alliance—Managing the Productivity/Technology Dilemma*, Harvard Business School Press.

Kast, F.E. and Rosenzweig, J.E. (1979), *Organization and Management: A Systems and Contingency Approach*, McGraw-Hill, New York.

Kearney Management Consultants (1984), The barriers and the opportunities of IT—a management perspective. Institute of Administrative Management and D.T.I.

Keen, P. and Scott-Morton, M. (1978), *Decision Support Systems: An Organizational Perspective*, Addison-Wesley, Reading, Mass.

Keen, P.G.W. (1981), 'Information systems and organizational change', *Communications of the Association for Computing Machinery*, **24**, No. 1.

Kempner, C.H. and Tregoe, B.B. (1965), *The Rational Manager*, McGraw-Hill, New York.

Khandwalla, P.N. (1974), 'Mass output orientation of operations technology and organizational structure', *Administrative Science Quarterly*, March.

— (1972), *Uncertainty and the Optimal Design of Organizations*, Faculty of Management Working Paper, McGill University, Montreal.

King, K.J. and Maryanski, F.J. (1983), 'Information management trends in office automation', *Proceedings of the IEEE*, **71**, No. 4, 514–28, April.

Klauss, R. and Bass, B.M. (1982), *International Communication in Organizations*, Academic Press.

Klingen, J.S. (1975), *Company strategy. A Managerial Approach for Strategic Control*, Saxon House, Farnborough, Hants.

Laing, G.J. (1980), 'Communication and its constraints on the structure of organizations', *Omega*, **8**, No. 3, 287–301.

Langlois, Ch. V. and Seignobos, Ch. (1898), *Introduction to the Study of History*, London.

Large, P. (1984), *The Micro-revolution Revisited*, Frances Pinter, London.

— (1980), *The Micro-revolution*, Fontana.

Laurie, P. (1983), *The Joy of Computers*, Hutchinson, London.

Lawrence, P. (1984), *Management in Action*, Routledge and Kegan Paul, London.

Lawrence, P.R. and Lorsch, J.W. (1967), *Organization and Environment*, Harvard Business School.

Leavitt, H. and Whisler, T. (1957), 'Management in the 1980s', *Harvard Business Review*, November/December.

Lewis, W.A. (1978), *Growth and Fluctuations, 1870–1913*, Allen and Unwin.

Liff, S. (1983), 'Monitoring technical change and employment', *Futures*, October.

Likert, R. (1961), *New Patterns of Management*, McGraw-Hill, New York.

Litterer, J.A. (1965), *The Analysis of Organizations*, John Wiley, New York.

Long, R.J. (1984), 'Microelectronic information technology and the office: human and organizational implications', Paper presented at the annual meeting of the British Sociological Association, Bradford, April.

Lorsch, J.W. and Allen III, S.A. (1973), *Managing Diversity and Interdependence*, Harvard Business School.

Lucas, H.C. (1982), *Information Systems Concepts for Management*, McGraw-Hill.

— and Sutton, J.A. (1977), 'The stage hypothesis and s-curve: some contradictory evidence', *Communications of the A.C.M.*, **20**, No. 4, 25–9.

Lucey, T. (1987), *Management Information Systems*, D.P. Publications, Eastleigh.

Macdonald Stuart, McLamberton, D. and Manderville, T.D. (eds) (1983), *The Trouble with Technology*, Frances Pinter, 1983.

Maddison, J. (1983), *Education in the Microelectronics Era*, Open University Press, Milton Keynes.

Madge, J. (1978), *The Tools of Social Science*, Longman.

Malcolm Warner (1984), *Microprocessors, Manpower and Society*, Gower, Aldershot.

March, J.G. and Simon, H.A. (1958), *Organizations*, John Wiley, New York.

Markus, M.I. (1983), 'Power, politics and M.I.S. implementation', *Communications of the A.C.M.*, **26**, No. 6, 430–44.

Marlow, H. (1975), *Managing Change: A Strategy of our Time*, Institute of Personnel Management, London.

Marsh, P. (1984), 'Why Normalair-Garnett became flexible, *Financial Times*, 1 March.

Maslow, A.H. (1945), *Motivation and Personality*, Harper, New York.

Martin, C.J. and Winch, G.W. (1984), 'Senior managers and computers', *Management Decision*, February.

McCall, M. *et al.* (1977), *Studies of Managerial Work: Results and Methods*, Technical Report 9, Smith Richardson Foundation, Centre for Creative Leadership.

McFarlan, F.W. and McKenney, J.L. (1983), 'The information archipelago— governing the new world', *Harvard Business Review*, **61**, No. 4, 91–9.

Menzies, H. (1981), *Women and the Chip*, Institute for Research on Public Policy, Montreal.

Menzies, H. (1982), *Computers on the Job: Surviving Canada's Microcomputer Revolution*, James Lorimer, Toronto.

Meyer, N.D. (1982), 'Office automation: a progress report', *Technology and People*, **1**, 107–21.

Miles, M.B. (1979), 'Qualitative data as an attractive nuisance: the problem of analysis', *Administrative Science Quarterly*, **24**, 590–601.

Miller, E.J. and Rice, A.K. (1967), *Systems of Organization*, Tavistock, London.

Mintzbserg, H. (1984), *Power in and Around Organizations*, Prentice Hall, New York.

— (1973), *The Nature of Managerial Work*, Harper and Row, New York.

— and McHugh, A. (1985), 'Strategy formation in an adhocracy', *Administrative Science Quarterly*, June.

Mitchell, T.R. (1985), 'An evaluation of the validity of correlational research conducted in organizations', *The Academy of Management Review*, **10**, No. 2.

Moto-Oka, T. (1982), *Fifth Generation Computer Systems*, North-Holland, Amsterdam.

Mumford, E. (1981), *Values, Technology and Work*, Martinus Nijhoff, Amsterdam.

— (1972), *Job Satisfaction: A Study of Computer Specialists*, Longmans, London.

— and Henshall, D. (1978), *A Participative Approach to the Design of Computer Systems*, Associated Business Press, London.

—, Land, F. and Hawgood, J. (1978), 'A participative approach to the design of computer systems', *Impact of Science on Society*, **28**, No. 3, 251–72.

Murray, W.J. (1984), *The British Telecom Digital Transmission Network*, IEE Conference Publication 235, 29–33.

Naughton, J. (1986), *Artificial Intelligence and Industrial Training*, Systems Group, The Open University.

Nelson, R. (1982), 'The role of knowledge in R and D efficiency, *Quarterly Journal of Economics*, **97**, No. 3, 453–70.

Newman, M. and Rosenberg, D. (1985), 'Systems analysis and the politics of organizational control', *Omega*, **13**, No. 5, 393–406.

Nolan, R.L. (1979), 'Managing the crisis in data processing', *Harvard Business Review*, March/April.

Nora, S. and Minc, A. (1978), *L'information de la Société*, Documentation Française, Paris.

Northcott, J. and Rogers P. (1982), *Microelectronics in .ndustry. What's Happening in Britain?*, Policy Studies Institute, London.

— and Rogers, P. (1984), *Microelectronics in British Industry: The Pattern of Change*, Policy Studies Institute, London.

Olson, M.H. (1980), *Organization of Information Services: Alternative Approaches*, UMI Research Press.

O'Neill, H.E. and Kubany, A.J. (1959), 'Observation methodology and supervisory behaviour', *Personnel Psychology*, **12**, 85–96.

O'Reilly, C. (1980), 'Individuals and information overload in organizations: is more necessarily better?', *Academy of Management Journal*, **23**.

Otway, H.J. and Peltu, M. (eds) (1984), *The Managerial Challenge of New Office Technology*, Butterworths, London.

— and Peltu, M. (eds) (1983), *New Office Technology: Human and Organizational Aspects*, Pinter, London.

P.E. Consulting Services (1986), *Attitudes and Acceptances of Information Technology*, London.

Parker, W.N. (1972), 'Technology resources and economic change in the West in A. Youngson (ed.), *Economic Development in the Long Run*, Allen and Unwin, London.

Pavitt, K. (ed.) (1980), *Technical Innovation and British Economic Performance*, Macmillan.

Peters, T.J. and Waterman, R.H. (1982), *In Search of Excellence*, Harper and Row.

Periera, B. (1984), 'The information technology bandwagon: planning for the late 1980s', Acuche managers' development course, Newcastle-Upon-Tyne Polytechnic (Mimeo).

Perrow, C. (1979), *Complex Organization: A Critical Essay*, 2nd edition, Scott, Foresman, Chicago.

— (1967), 'A framework for the comparative analysis of organizations', *American Sociological Review*, **32**, 194–208.

Pettigrew, A., Jones, G. and Reason, P. (1982), *Training and Development Roles on their Organizational Setting*, Training Studies, Manpower Services Commission, London.

Pfeffer, J. (1982), *Organizaions and Organization Theory*, Pitman, Marshfield, Maine.

Piercy, Nigel and Evans, Martin (1983), *Managing Marketing Information*, Croom Helm, London.

Piercy, Nigel (1984a), 'How to manage I.T.', *Management Today*.

— (ed.) (1984b), *The Management Implications of Information Technology*, Croom Helm, London.

Piore, M.J. and Sabel, C.F. (1984), *The Second Industrial Divide*, Basic Books, New York.

Platt, J. (1976), *The Realities of Research*, University of Sussex Press, London.

Porat, M.V. (1976), 'The Information Economy', Ph.D. Thesis, Department of Communication, Stamford University.

Potterdam Conference Papers, International Symposium on Fifth Generation and Super Computers, Potterdam, December.

Preece, D.A. (1986) in C.A. Voss (ed.), *Managing Advanced Manufacturing Technology*, Proceedings of the UK Operations Management Association Conference 2–3 January, 1986, I.F.S. (Publications), Berlin.

Pugh, D.S., Hickson, D.J., Hinings, C.R. and Turner, C. (1968), 'Dimensions of organisation structure', *Admin. Science Quarterly*, **13**, 65–105.

Raitt, D. (1982), *New Information Technology—Social Aspects, Usage and Trends*, Proceedings of the 5th International Online Information Meeting, London, 8–10 December, 1981, Oxford.

Rajan Amin (1985), *Recruitment and Training Effects of Technical Change*, Institute of Manpower Studies, London.

Ray, G.F. (1983), 'The diffusion of mature technologies', NIESR Economic Review, No. 106.

Reason, P. and Rowan, J. (eds) (1981), *Human Inquiry: A Sourcebook of New Paradym Research*, J. Wiley and Sons.

Rosenberg, N. (1976), *Perspectives on Technology*, Cambridge University Press, Cambridge.

Rosenthal, R. and Rosnow, R. (eds.) (1970), *Sources of Artifact in Social Research*, Academic Press, New York.

Rothwell, S. (1984), 'Supervisors and new technology', *Employment Gazette*, 21–4, January.

Russell, P. (1982), *The Awakening Earth—Our Next Revolutionary Leap*, Routledge.

Sadlier, C.D. (1980), 'Office of the future—new challenges for operational research', *Omega*, **8**, No. 1, 21–8.

Salvaggio, J.L. (1983), 'Social problems of computer societies', *Telecommunication Policy*, 228–42, September.

Sayles, L.R. (1964), *Managerial Behavior: Administration in Complex Organizations*, McGraw-Hill, New York.

Schuler, R.S. and Blank, L.F. 'Relationships among types of communication, organizational level, and employee satisfaction and performance', *IEEE Transactions on Engineering Management*, **23**, No. 3, 124–9.

Schein, E. (1984), 'Coming to a new awareness of organizational culture', *Sloan Management Review*, Winter.

— (1969), *Process Consultation: Its Role in Organization Development*, Addison-Wesley, Reading, Mass.

Schmookler, J. (1966), *Invention and Economic Growth*, Harvard University Press, Cambridge, Mass.

Schumann, G. (1984), 'The macro and micro economic and social impact of advanced computer technology', *Futures*, **16**, No. 3.

Schumpeter, J. (1954), *History of Economic Analysis*, Oxford University Press, New York.

— (1939), *Business Cycles*, McGraw-Hill, New York.

Scott, B.R. (1971), *Stages of Corporate Development*, Harvard Business School.

Senker, P.J. (1984), *Learning to Use Micro-electronics. A Review of Empirical Research on the Implications of Micro-electronics for Work Organizations, Skills, and Industrial Relations*, NEDC Office, London.

Shannon, C.E. and Weaver, W. (1949), *The Mathematical Theory of Communication*, University of Illinois Press, Urbana.

Simon, H. (1965), *The Shape of Automation for Men and Management*, Harper and Row, New York.

Simons, G.L. (1983), *Towards Fifth Generation Computers*, NCC Publications, Manchester.

Singer, C.J. (ed.) (1954–8), *A History of Technology*, Vols. I–V, Oxford University Press.

Smith, H. (1975), *Strategies of Social Research: The Methodological Imagination*, Prentice Hall.

Smith, Roger B. (1984), 'Future technology and the automotive industry', *Proceedings of International Conference on Future Development in Technology. The Year 2,000*, London, April.

Smith, S. (1985), 'A political economy of urbanisation and state structure; urban and industrial change in two selected areas. PhD. thesis, University of Kent.

Sorge, A., Hartmann, G., Warner, M. and Nicholas, I. (1983), *Microelectronics and Manpower in Manufacturing*, Gower, Aldershot.

—, Hartmann, G., Warner, M. and Nicholas, I. (1982), 'Technology, organization and manpower in N. Bjorn-Anderson, M. Earl, O. Holst and E. Mumford (eds), *Information Society: For Richer, For Poorer*, North-Holland, Amsterdam.

Starbuck, W.H. (ed.) (1979), *Handbook of Organizational Design*, Volume 1, Elsevier.

Stewart, R. (1976), *Contrasts in Management*, McGraw-Hill, London.

— (1971), *How Computers Affect Management*, Pan Books, London.

— (1967), *Managers and their Jobs*, Macmillan, London.

Storey, J. (1987), 'The management of new office technology: choice, control and social structure in the insurance industry, *Journal of Management Studies*, **24**, 1 January.

Strandh, A. (1979), *A History of the Machine*, A. and W. Publications, New York.

Swann, Lord (1983), 'Forward', *Annual Report of the Technical Change Centre*, London.

Swords-Isherwood, N. and Senke, P. (1978), 'Automation in the engineering industry', *Labour Research*, **67**.

Taylor, F.W. (1911), *Principles and Methods of Scientific Management*, Harper, New York.

Teece, D. (1980), 'The diffusion of an administration innovation', *Management Science*, **26**, No. 5, 464–70.

Thomas, D.G. (1986), *Survey of Engineering Firms in South Wales*, EITB New Technology Report, July, (Mimeo).

Thompson, J.P. (1967), *Organizations in Action*, McGraw-Hill, New York.

Toffler, Alvin (1970), *Future Shock*, Bodley Head, London.

Toothill, G.C. (1965), *Electronic Computers*, Penguin, Harmondsworth.

Towill, D.R. (1984), 'A production engineering approach to robot selection', *Omega*, **12**, No. 3.

Toynbee, A. (1908), *Lectures on the Industrial Revolution of Eighteenth Century England*, Longmans Green, London.

Tricker, R.I. (1982), *Effective Information Management*, Beaumont Executive Press, Oxford.

Trist, E.L., Higgin, G.W., Murray, H. and Pollack, A.B. (1963), *Organizational Choice*, Tavistock, London.

Tsichritzis, D.C. and Lochovsky, F.H. (1980), 'Office information systems: challenge for the '80s', *Proceedings of the IEEE*, **68**, No. 9, 1054–9.

Tynan, O. (1984), 'Change and the nature of work', Work Research Unit, November (Mimeo).

Uhlig, R.P., Farber, D.J. and Bair, J.H. (1979), *The Office of the Future*, North-Holland, Amsterdam.

Urwick, L. and Brech, E.F.L. (1947), *The Making of Scientific Management, Volume III: The Hawthorne Investigations*, Sir Isaac Pitman and Sons, London.

Voss, C.A. (1986), 'Managing advanced manufacturing technology', *Proceedings of the UK Operations Management Association Conference*, 2–3 January, IFS Publications, Berlin.

Walker, R. (1986), 'Computer sytems architecture', Luton College of Higher Education (Mimeo).

Warner, Malcolm (1984), *Microprocessors, Manpower and Society*, Gower, Aldershot.

Watson, J.M. (1985), 'The technology that makes I.T. possible—computers', *Journal of the Institute of Electrical Engineers*, 15–18, January.

Webb, S. and B. (1932), *Methods of Social study*, Cambridge University Press, London.

Webb *et al.* (1967), *Unobtrusive Measures*, Rand McNally.

Weick, K. (1968), 'Systematic observational methods', in Lindzey and Aronson, *Handbook of social Psychology*, Volume 2. Addison Wesley, Reading, Mass.

Whisler, T.J. (1966), 'The impact of advanced technology on management decision making' in J. Steiber (ed.), *Employment Problems of Automation and Advanced Technology: An International Prospectus*, Macmillan, London.

White, G. (1983), *Re-design of Work Organizations—I.T.'s Impact on Supervisors*, Work Research Unit Report 8, London.

Wiener, M.J. (1981), *English Culture and the Decline of the Industrial Spirit, 1850–1980*, Cambridge University Press, Cambridge.

Wilkinson, B. (1983), *The Shop Floor Politics of New Technology*, Heineman, London.

— (1982), 'New technology and human tasks: the future of work in manufacturing industry in L. Bannon *I.T. Impact on the Way of Life*, Tycooly, Dublin.

— and Smith S. (1984), 'From old school hunches to departmental lunches', *Sociological Review*, February.

Williams, B. (1983), *The Economic Impact of Science and Technology in Historical Perspective*, The Technical Change Centre, London, June.

Williams, B. (1983), *Living Better with Technology*, The Technical Change Centre, London, February.

— (1981), *Industry and Technical Progress Revisited*, The Technical Change Centre, London, April.

Winch, G. (ed.) (1983), *Information Technology in Manufacturing Processes: Case Studies in Technological Change*, Rossendale, London.

Wood, S. (ed.) (1982), *The Degradation of Work?* Hutchinson, London.

Woodward, J. (1965), *Industrial Organizations: Theory and Practice*, Oxford University Press.

— (1958), *Management and Technology*, Tavistock Institute, London.

Wright-Mills, C. (1959), *The Sociological Imagination*, Oxford University Press, New York.

Wynne, B. (1983), in H.J. Otway and M. Peltu (eds), *The Changing Roles of Managers*, Frances Pinter, London.

— and Otway, H.J. (1982), 'Information technology: power and managers in E. Bjorn-Anderson (eds), *Information Society: For Richer, For Poorer*, North-Holland, Amsterdam.

Yap, C.S. (1984), 'A framework for the analysis of the information characteristics of organizations, Cambridge University Engineering Department (Mimeo).

Yukl, G.A. and Nemeroff, W. (1979), 'Identification and measurement of specific categories of leadership behaviour: measurement progress report', in J.G. Hunt and L.L. Larson (eds), *Cross Currents in Leadership*, Southern Illinois University Press, Carbondale.

Zweig, F. (1948), *Labour, Life and Poverty*, Gollancz, London.

Index

The index is arranged alphabetically word by word. A page reference followed by 'f' indicates a figure in the text. IT is used as an abbreviation for Information Technology.